The Daily Telegraph

YORKSHIRE DALES

in a week

MIKE GERRARD

D0784476

Headway · Hodder & Stoughton

Acknowledgements

The author and publishers are grateful to the following for permission to reproduce photographs in this volume:

J Allan Cash Ltd: Front cover; Bradford Economic Development Unit: p 111; Yorkshire & Humberside Tourist Board: pp 61, 87, 88, 92

All other photographs taken by the author

Maps created by Alan Gilliland and Glenn Swann

Front cover: Swaledale looking towards Melbecks Moor
Back cover: Stained glass in the Parish Church of All Saints, Ilkley

British Library Cataloguing in Publication Data
Gerrard, Mike
"Daily Telegraph" Yorkshire Dales in a Week
("Daily Telegraph" Travel in a Week Series)
I. Title II. Series
914.28404

ISBN 0 340 58313 4

First published 1993
Impression number   10 9 8 7 6 5 4 3 2
Year   1998   1997   1996   1995   1994   1993

© 1993 The Telegraph plc

All rights reserved. No part of this publication may be reproduced or transmitted in any form or by any means, electronic or mechanical, including photocopy, recording, or any information storage and retrieval system, without permission in writing from the publisher or under licence from the Copyright Licensing Agency Limited. Further details of such licences (for reprographic reproduction) may be obtained from the Copyright Licensing Agency Limited, of 90 Tottenham Court Road, London WIP 9HE.

Printed in Italy for the educational publishing division of Hodder & Stoughton Ltd, Mill Road, Dunton Green, Sevenoaks, Kent TN 13 2YA by New Interlitho, Milan.

YORKSHIRE DALES IN A WEEK

Introduction

This guide is designed for visitors touring the Yorkshire Dales who wish to see the best of its scenic beauty and visitor attractions in the limited time at their disposal. We have divided the Dales into seven areas, each of which can easily be covered in a day's drive. Within each of these 'Days' the most interesting sights, from the summits of the Three Peaks and underground caverns to country houses and the prettiest villages, have been listed as a menu of options, arranged in alphabetical order for easy reference. From the Day's menu you can choose the attractions which hold most appeal, depending on the weather, your interests, and whether you are travelling with children. Symbols placed alongside the text will aid you in your choice.

The Dales are, of course, the valleys that run between the high hills, ranging from the most famous, Wensleydale, to delightful smaller dales such as Kingsdale. They receive over 10 million visitors a year and the aim of this guide is to give a critical appraisal of the most popular tourist honeypots and help you discover some of the region's hidden gems. Our assessments of the different sights and attractions will give you a clear idea of what you can expect to see, the best time of day and year to pay a visit and, where admission is charged, whether the attractions offer value for money. As well as covering the main towns and tourist attractions, we have highlighted small gems in each area including craft studios, art galleries, factory shops and good places for lunch.

A walk of the day in each area is described in detail. Some are just over an hour long and provide an opportunity to get out of the car and stretch your legs; others are longer and more strenuous but the views are worth the effort. At the end of each Day we have given suggestions for places to stay, from country house hotels to superior bed and breakfast, and places to eat, from restaurants offering fine dining to pubs serving good home-made fare and Yorkshire ales.

CONTENTS

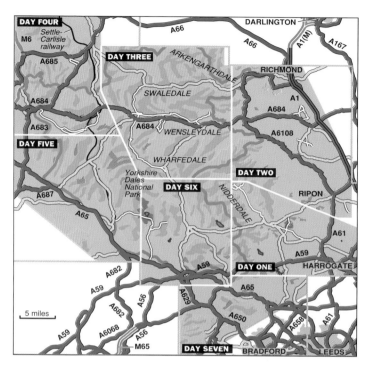

KEY TO SYMBOLS

⭐ Star Attraction

☆ Well worth a visit

☆ Of interest

❗ Walk of the day

---- Route of walk

☀ Fine weather attraction

🌧 Wet weather attraction

🏃 Enjoyable for children

ⓘ Tourist Information Centre

⬤ Lunch/snack stop

🏠 Hotel

Ĝ Guesthouse

✘ Restaurant

🍺 Pub with good food

🍺 Pub with accommodation

🏃5 Children allowed (number = from which age)

🐕 Dogs allowed

▭ Credit cards accepted

⊠ Credit cards not accepted

£ Bed and breakfast under £17 per person; three-course meal under £10 a head

££ Bed and breakfast £18-£35 per person; three-course meal £11-£16 a head

£££ Bed and breakfast £36-£49 per person; three-course meal £17-£24 a head

££££ Bed and breakfast over £50 per person; three-course meal over £25 a head

HARROGATE AND THE SOUTH-EAST DALES

The Regency spa town of Harrogate, with its wealth of accommodation, attractions and restaurants, is a good base for exploring this corner of the Dales. The scenery here is gentle rather than dramatic, but it has its unique attractions, such as the brooding Brimham Rocks.

Harrogate offers plenty to do, whatever the weather. On a wet day, take in the shops, the museum, pamper yourself with a Turkish bath and a visit to Betty's tea rooms, or, if you have children, visit the 9-pin bowling alley. If the weather is fine, join with a town tour or walk to the Harlow Carr Gardens where in half-an-hour or so you'll be on the edge of town, looking at open country.

A good family day out could include Knaresborough in the morning – Wednesday and Saturday are market days – and Ripley Castle in the afternoon. If the weather is uncertain, head for Stump Cross Caverns then take in Pateley Bridge's Nidderdale Museum after lunch. Make the most of fine weather by visiting How Stean Gorge and Brimham Rocks, perhaps having lunch at The Sportsman's Arms in Wath-in-Nidderdale, from where there are a couple of pleasant country strolls.

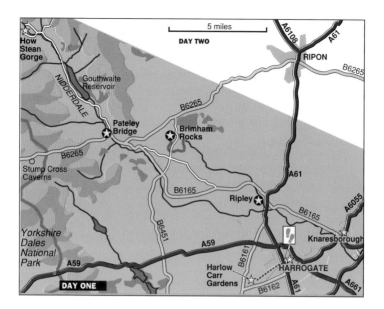

BRIMHAM ROCKS

The name Brimham aptly suggests the brooding gritstone nature of these rocks that jut up from the surrounding moorland like giant Henry Moore sculptures. From the car park (where there's a small charge) several paths lead through the rocks to the National Trust Visitors' Centre, with its viewing platform. On a clear day you can see... well, as far as Cleveland anyway. At the Centre buy *Brimham Rocks, Nidderdale*, by Geoff Hall, one of the wardens. This booklet suggests several walks and has interesting information about the sculpting of these rocks, shaped over millions of years into strange and sometimes familiar forms – the blacksmith and anvil are easily spotted. Covering 387 acres, this surreal moorland landscape is not to be missed – Emily Brontë meets Salvador Dali.

Brimham Rocks, Summerbridge, Harrogate (between the B6165 and B6265 roads).
Tel: 0423-780688
Opening times: 11am-5pm - Apr 8-May 24, weekends and Bank Hols only; Mar 29-
Apr 7 and May 25-Oct 31 daily; Nov 1-Mar 28 closed
Admission: parking charge £1

Brimham Rocks

☆ HARROGATE

Harrogate has been a spa town for over 400 years, the kind of place (like Cheltenham or Bath) you expect to find in the genteel south of England, not in rugged Yorkshire, a few miles north of industrialised Leeds and Bradford. But combine northern hospitality with turn-of-the-century charm and hundreds of acres of parkland, and you have a very pleasant town. Its Victorian buildings, arcades, antique shops and air of respectability have made it the butt of jokes, but its residents don't mind. As one said: 'We've lived in Harrogate for 18 years and my wife still thinks we're on holiday.' In more recent years the town has developed as an international conference centre, and the hotels and restaurants have raised their standards to meet this demand.

To familiarise yourself with Harrogate, try one of the free **Guided Walks** organised by the local Tourist Office. These informative walks of an hour or so are conducted by local historians, who tend to be interested in the minutiae of life and can chat about everything from sewers to adultery in an informal way that makes the past come alive. 'We know,' one said, 'that Hales Bar – which I can heartily recommend – has been there since at least the 17th century, as the landlord then was reported for drilling through from his cellar into the basement of the spa across the road and selling the spa waters.' There are several themed walks to choose from, starting outside the Royal Pump Room Museum and operating from spring to autumn, but days and times vary according to the availability of the volunteer guides. Get up-to-date details from the **Tourist Information Centre** in the Royal Baths Assembly Rooms in Crescent Road (tel: 0423-525666).

At **Hales Bar** in Crescent Road, opposite the Pump Room Museum, gas-burning lamps on the counter of the large bar on the right give the place an intimate Victorian atmosphere. Don't equate that with romantic, as this is a down-to-earth place. Food is served every day from noon-2pm and 5.30-9.30pm (though usually available until closing time). In addition to sandwiches there are hearty home-made standards like steak and kidney pie, chicken and mushroom pie and giant Yorkshire pudding with roast beef.

The Royal Pump Room Museum was built in 1842 to house the Old Sulphur Well, and this small octagonal building with its copper dome is now the Museum and a Harrogate landmark. Inside is an interesting rather than essential collection: Harrogate's Last Bath Chair, more buttonhooks than you knew existed and a small bicycle collection. There are some delights worth truffling out, like old cinema and theatre posters and a model of 'Old Betty', who dispensed sulphur water from a Harrogate well for 60 years – using the same beaker. Before leaving, try a free sample (in a clean glass) of the spa water which still rises beneath the building.

The Royal Pump Room Museum, Royal Parade, Harrogate. Tel: 0423-503340
Opening times: daily except Dec 25, 26 and Jan 1, Mon-Sat 10am-5pm, Sun 2-5pm
Admission: adult £1.10; child 55p

Harrogate – Pump Room Museum and Harlow Carr Botanical Gardens

FROM PUMP ROOM TO HARLOW CARR GARDENS

There's an enjoyable 1½ mile walk from the Pump Room Museum through the Valley Gardens to reach the Harlow Carr Gardens on the edge of town, which should take a leisurely 45 minutes. Harrogate is rightly proud of the many parks and gardens that make the town centre such a pleasant place. As well as floral displays, the Valley Gardens have crazy golf, pitch and putt, tennis courts and a playground – so allow more time if you're easily diverted, or have children.

With the Pump Room Museum behind you, walk through the main entrance to the Valley Gardens and take the lower path which leads past the fountain. Pass the tennis courts on your left and as you approach the woods look out for the war memorial in the trees on your right. Here leave the main path and follow the track to the right that goes into the pine woods. In these woods there are plenty of birds to watch for, like coal tits, robins and willow warblers, with goldcrests twittering high in the conifers.

Cross Harlow Moor Road, continue along the path, and you reach an open grassy area. Go straight ahead, keeping the grass on your left, and rejoin an asphalt path. There are lovely open views to the right of the rolling green of Harlow Moor, a refreshing view of countryside so close to the town. This path then heads straight on to Crag Lane, emerging almost opposite the entrance to the 68-acre Harlow Carr Gardens.

 The **Harlow Carr Gardens** belong to the Northern Horticultural Society and are a pleasant place to sit, walk or picnic – and admire the well-labelled collection of plants and trees. The layout is a mix of the neat and the natural, with a variety of pathways, hedges, streams, woods and lawns, and a wild wood marking the boundary on one side. A special interest garden includes a Killarney strawberry tree and a Chinese privet, plus a historic collection of old plants.

Old gardening tools aren't forgotten, either. The Museum of Gardening isn't much bigger than a garden shed, and equally crammed with an odd collection of items: thistle cutters, weed grubbers, 'The Dandy Dibber' and rhubarb forcing pots. There's also a collection of lawnmowers. Did you know that the lawnmower was invented in 1830? This begs the question as to which came first, the lawnmower or the lawn?

The gardens are peaceful, and large enough not to be crowded on a summer afternoon, though weekends are best avoided. As well as a place for wandering, and bemoaning the state of your own garden, it's also a place to sit and relax. A light and airy cafeteria offers tea, cakes and simple cooked meals, plus a lovely view of the gardens.

Harlow Carr Gardens, Crag Lane, Harrogate. Tel: 0423-565418
Opening times: daily, Nov-Mar 9am till dusk, Mar-Oct 9am-7.30pm or dusk if earlier.
Museum closes 4.30pm
Admission: adult £2.50; accompanied children free

One of Harrogate's late 19th-century attractions is **The Harrogate Turkish and Sauna Suite**, just the place for a few hours of unashamed self-indulgence. Looking grimly Victorian from the outside, inside the atmosphere is more of the timeless Orient, with tiled rooms of elaborate design. The predominant grey and pale blue patterns are soothing, and the Suite offers a Russian Steam Room, Cold Plunge Room, three Hot Rooms of varying temperatures and a Massage/Shampoo Room. Finally there's an ornate Rest Room, with drinks and newspapers, the kind of place to lie back and relax in before facing the world again. The rooms are communal, with rows of beds to lie on, but they're not crammed together and there's usually space enough for privacy.

If you haven't been to a sauna before then don't be nervous as the staff will explain everything. Start with a shower and hot sauna, before plunging into the cold pool. This can be repeated a few times before moving on to an optional massage. Ignore the salacious connotations these things have in Britain, as the genuine article makes you feel wonderfully healthy and clean, and at peace with the world. Towels and robes are provided, and if you wish to wear a swimsuit then no one will mind, though with most people unselfconsciously naked you'll probably prefer to do the same. There are no mixed sessions - yet.

The Harrogate Turkish and Sauna Suite, Crescent Road, Harrogate (but use the entrance in Parliament Street). Tel: 0423-562498
Opening times: Ladies - 1-9pm Tues and Thurs, 9am-12.30pm Fri, 9am-5pm Sun;
Men - 1-9pm Mon, Wednes & Fri, 9am-12.30pm Tues, 9am-5pm Sat
Admission: Sauna or Solarium £2.50; Turkish Bath and Sauna £5.50

A contrast to a peaceful sauna is a boisterous visit to the **Kegelbahn 9-pin Bowl**. The place is impeccably clean and well-run; the emphasis is on family entertainment and it can become quite noisy. The game comes from Germany, with a lighter ball and shorter alley than conventional 10-pin bowling, making it easier for younger children to join in. There are ten lanes – book in advance to be safe – with up to ten players per lane. It's cheaper on weekdays before 6pm, and shoes can be hired but trainers are acceptable. Under-14s must be accompanied by an adult, and there's no eating, drinking or smoking around the lanes. A large café/bar area provides a wide choice of inexpensive fast-food meals, many with a German flavour: Nudel Auflauf, Schweinerippe and Kegelwurst in Yorkshire (herb sausages, spicy sauce and a Yorkshire pudding!).

Kegelbahn 9-pin Bowl, Tower Street, Harrogate. Tel: 0423-529191
Opening times: Mon-Sat 10am-midnight, Sun 10am-11.30pm. Last entry: one hour
before closing time
Admission: Lane charge £10 an hour weekdays, £12 evenings and weekends

☆ HOW STEAN GORGE

A lovely drive alongside Gouthwaite Reservoir leads to this area known as Yorkshire's Little Switzerland. It centres round a narrow limestone gorge up to 80ft deep that's pretty without being spectacular. Access is along walkways and bridges which take you from side to side of How Stean Beck as it cuts its way through, creating a few small waterfalls as it goes. The damp rocky walls support an abundance of ferns and plants, such as ox tongue and wild garlic, as well as primroses in the spring. The bird life is plentiful, with dippers and various finches to be seen. There are many caves in the land around the gorge, and it's a good place for exploring – but dangerous, so beware. Children love going into Tom Taylor's cave, over 500ft long, where a hoard of Roman coins was found in the 19th century. Take a torch to save hiring one at the café, which is where you also buy your ticket. There is free parking, and a children's play area. The booklet and map are recommended, as the area away from the gorge is surprisingly flat, several of the caves being no more than holes in the ground and hard to spot from a distance.

Gouthwaite Reservoir, Nidderdale

The **How Stean Gorge Café** offers terrific value: the kind of place where a plate of sausage, bacon, egg and chips qualifies as a 'light snack' on the menu. A real meal would be home-made beef pie, Yorkshire pudding, potatoes and two veg. No one should be surprised to find Death by Chocolate among the puddings. The building is a large pine lodge with plenty of basic refectory-style seating, mostly at tables for four, with brisk service.

How Stean Gorge, Lofthouse, near Harrogate. Tel: 0423-755666
Opening times: the Gorge is always accessible, the Café open 10am-6pm every day
except Christmas and the day of the Pateley Bridge Show in late Sept
Admission: adult £1; child 50p

☆ KNARESBOROUGH

Steep streets rise up from the River Nidd and lead to the heart of Knaresborough with its church, castle ruins and market square, where you'll find the oldest chemist's shop in the country, dating from 1256. The castle is a century older, and was one of King John's favourites. With old street names like Jockey Lane and Water Bag Bank, a grand 19th-century viaduct and a bustling atmosphere, Knaresborough feels lived in, not a twee tourist town, though it's certainly popular with visitors.

The Knaresborough **Tourist Information Centre** at 35 Market Place (tel: 0423-866886) is open from April to mid-October.

9

How Stean Gorge, Nidderdale   *River Nidd, Knaresborough*

Watch out for the Town Crier who opens the market at 11am on Wednesdays and Saturdays, and appears again outside the castle at 3pm to make the day's announcements. The lively, colourful market sells mainly local fruit, vegetables and flowers, as well as jeans, music tapes and shoes.

A popular attraction is **Mother Shipton's Cave**, the car entrance being by the High Bridge on the Harrogate Road, with another entrance for pedestrians only on the A59 by Low Bridge. Knaresborough is woefully short of parking space, especially on market days, so if you plan to visit the cave anyway you can park your car here, leave it all day and come and go as you please. Sensible thinking by the owners, which helps compensate for the rather high admission charge.

Set in 12 acres of undulating woodlands alongside the river, the cave itself is a good ten-minute walk from the car park, although the wide track allows disabled visitors to drive almost up to it. The amusing and informative guided tours set off twice an hour and last about 30 minutes. In the 15th century this area was a remote part of a larger forest, with a reputation for magic, and it was in this cave that Mother Shipton was born to a runaway peasant girl. The child was deformed, and grew up to gain a rep-

Petrified toys in Mother Shipton's Cave, Knaresborough

utation for prophecy, writing for example: 'Water shall come over Ouze Bridge, and a windmill shall be set upon a tower, and an Elm Tree shall lie at every man's door.' When, many years later, the city of York acquired a piped water system, the water did flow over Ouze Bridge, being drawn up by a windmill, and the water was conducted to houses in pipes made from hollowed-out trees – elm trees! Many more prophecies are explained in a colourful and fascinating booklet. Alongside the cave is the Petrifying Well, where minerals in the dripping water turn objects to stone. It's now mostly done for charity and a museum displays a collection of such items, ranging from Queen Mary's slipper to Sid Little's underpants. A petrifying thought, indeed.

Mother Shipton's Cave, Prophesy House, The High Bridge, Knaresborough.
Tel: 0423-864600
Opening times: Easter-Oct daily, 9.30am-5.30pm (last admission 5pm), in winter Sun only, 10am-5pm (last admission 4pm). These times may vary slightly in future
Admission: adult £3.30; child 5-17 £2.20

Mother Shipton's Inn, round the corner at the Low Bridge exit, is friendly and cosy inside, with a lively mix of locals and visitors. There's a beer garden at the back, with views across the river to Knaresborough Castle. It serves Theakston's and Younger's beers and good food: a giant Yorkshire pudding with onion gravy and a slice of roast beef, steak pies, home-made soups. Food is available noon-2pm; 7-9.30pm.

Knaresborough Castle consists mainly of its grand walls and a few crumbling rooms, with guides on hand to answer questions. Lawns have been laid inside the walls, with a small putting green and park benches looking down on the river. The most interesting feature is the subterranean Sallyport, an escape route from the castle which emerges some distance away. This opens for a brief guided tour every 20 minutes.

The Castle also contains the **Old Courthouse Museum**, small but good on local characters like Robert Floore (1160-1218), who lived in a Knaresborough cave having decided that a Cistercian monastery was too luxurious. A model of Old Mother Shipton is displayed, the museum's historian concluding that 'the idea that she was a monstrously ugly witch is sheer fabrication'. This is nicely at odds with what the guides at the Cave tell you! Another Knaresborough notable was Blind Jack, who was blinded by smallpox at six but still became a quantity surveyor, grew to be over 6ft tall and 17 stone, and died at the age of 93 leaving 90 great- and great-great-grandchildren. They don't make them like that any more.

Opening times: daily Easter-end Sept, 10.30am to 5pm
Admission: Castle 70p; Museum free

> Knaresborough's Finkle Street offers some superior shopping. **The Gordon Reece Gallery** is a kilim shop and art gallery (open Mon-Sat 10.30am-5pm, tel: 0423-866219). **Woodworker David Bailes** has a showroom on one side of the street and a workshop on the other where you can watch him at work, perhaps making his speciality, the grand-father clock (open Mon-Sat 9am-5pm, tel: 0423-868438).

✪ PATELEY BRIDGE

Pateley Bridge would be a pleasant but unexceptional place to pass through, if it were not for the excellent **Nidderdale Museum**, which demands a stop. Ask for directions at the **Tourist Information Centre** - a small kiosk in the main South-lands Car Park, at the bottom of the High Street (tel: 0423-711147, summer season only). The museum is a tiny gem of a place, tucked away in an old Victorian workhouse behind St Cuthbert's Church and with its own free car park. Winner of a National Heritage Museum of the Year Award in 1990, this jumble of delights seems to contain everything that anyone who ever lived in Nidderdale has ever owned: a Methodist teapot, a photo of the Pateley Bridge Ladies Cricket Team of 1898, a history of shaving from 1825 to the present day. Do not miss the scale model of four cottages from nearby Shaw Mills, furnished as they were in 1851, with the census returns beneath listing the occupants, from the elderly couple living alone at number 38 to the lodging house next door where 19 Irish teenagers lived, all working in the mills.

Nidderdale Museum, Pateley Bridge. Tel: 0423-711225
Opening times: 2-5pm - Oct-Easter, Sun only; Easter-Spring Bank Hol, weekends only; summer daily
Admission: adult 80p; child 40p

A few miles out of Pateley Bridge are the **Stump Cross Caverns**, which are not the best caves in the Dales but worth knowing about for a wet day. Children will enjoy looking for the shaped rocks: a sleeping cat, the Policeman's Truncheon, the Sandcastle Grotto or the Hawk. Don't go down if you have a bad back, as you must walk like Groucho Marx to duck under some low ceilings. The Caverns are best known for the finds of animal bones – reindeer, wolves, bison – now in London's Natural History Museum. There's a cafeteria with basic dishes like lasagne or fish and chips, as well as a souvenir shop selling rocks, fossils and general gifts. Admission is pricey for what you get: a self-guided underground tour of about 30 minutes, and extra for the guidebook.

Stump Cross Caverns, Greenhow Hill, Pateley Bridge. Tel: 0756-752780
Opening times: Easter-Nov, 10am-dusk; winter Sun only 11am-4pm
Admission: adult £2.40; child £1.20

✪ RIPLEY

Ripley's unusual appeal lies in the fact that a francophile Lord of the Manor rebuilt this tiny village in 1827, modelling it on a typical French village from Alsace-Lorraine. Even the village hall carries the inscription 'Hotel de Ville'. With its 15th-century parish church, saddlery, farm museum, and good food at the Boar's Head pub, Ripley is a thoroughly enjoyable place.

Ripley Castle has been home to the Ingilby family since 1320 and the present owners are Sir Thomas and Lady Ingilby. The Castle is really a stately home – small battlements, no high walls or dungeons – and the guided tour includes many of the rooms the family uses when it is not open to the public. Parts of the castle have been rebuilt and extended, and the rooms range from the mediaeval Knight's Chamber, with its panelled walls and ceiling and displays of swords and armour, to fine Georgian drawing rooms in turquoise and white. The tone of the guides is light and easy-going. Far from a 'hands-off' approach, visitors are encouraged to use the chairs – then told they're invaluable Chippendale originals. You will see a secret stairway and a priest's hole and hear a fascinating tale of the night Oliver Cromwell spent here. The tours run at regular intervals according to numbers, and last about an hour. Try to get there when it opens because crowds build up on busy days in this popular spot.

Ripley Castle, Ripley. Tel: 0423-770152
Opening times: Gardens - daily Mar 29-Oct 31, 11.30am-4.30pm; Castle - Good Fri,
Easter and Bank Hols Apr-Oct 11am-4.30pm, Apr and Oct Sat and Sun 11.30am-
4.30pm, May Tues-Thurs, Sat and Sun 2-4.30pm, June-Sept, Tues-Thurs, Sat and Sun
11.30am-4.30pm
Admission: adult £3.50; child £1.75

Ripley Castle

WHERE TO STAY

Burnt Yates

🖕 🧍 🐕 ✉ ££

High Winsley Cottage, *Burnt Yates,
near Harrogate, N Yorks HG3 3EP*
Tel: 0423-770662
Open all year
At the end of a long gated road you
may start to worry as you head for
what seems to be a solitary farm, but
tucked away to one side is High
Winsley Cottage. The owners are
heartily friendly and grow their own
fruit and veg, with free-range eggs for
breakfast and local game or home-bred
beef for dinner. The rooms are large
and comfortable, with double and twin
rooms at one end of the house suitable
for families. All have en suite bathrooms, tea-making facilities, comfy
armchairs, electric blankets and
Sanderson or Laura Ashley decor.

Harrogate

🖕 🧍 ☐ ££

Alexa House, *26 Ripon Road,
Harrogate HG2 2JJ*
Tel: 0423-501988
Open all year
Alexa House is a large 1830 detached
house, standing well back from the
main Ripon road and a five-minute
walk from the town centre. With 12
rooms and two self-contained suites, it
falls somewhere between hotel and
guesthouse, the rooms having hair-
dryers and clock radio as well as colour
TV and tea-making facilities. The
rooms are spacious enough, but some
would look even bigger without the
busy floral wallpaper and carpets, and
a few have en suite bathrooms
squeezed in, with the occasional
shower cubicle stuck in a corner. But all
are clean and pleasant, and the
hospitality of the hosts counts for a lot.

Harrogate

🖕 🧍 ✉ ££

Fountains Hotel, *27 Kings Road,
Harrogate HG1 5JY*
Tel: 0423-530483
Open all year
In a long tree-lined road of large
Victorian houses close to the town centre, many of them offering accommodation, Fountains Hotel comes with several local recommendations. The seven
rooms match some in hotels costing
twice the price. You forgo extras like
telephones and trouser presses, but all
rooms have colour TV and tea-making
facilities. The decor tends to the white
and bright, and the welcome from the
cheerful owner is Yorkshire hospitality
personified. 'I do an evening meal if
people want it, but I don't push it
because I've found people like to drive
out somewhere and get a pub meal...
and there must be a dozen good eating
places within five minutes' walk.'

Harrogate

🛏 ✕ 🧍 🐕 ☐ ££££

Grants Hotel, *Swan Road,
Harrogate HG1 2SS*
Tel: 0423-560666
*Open all year; Chimney Pots Restaurant
dinner only*
Looking like a row of Georgian terraces
from the outside, the inside of Grants
has been modernised to turn it into a
fine example of a smart small hotel.
There are 37 rooms, eight with suitable
access for the disabled. The staff
combine extreme friendliness with the
efficiency that business visitors
demand. Rooms are light, bright and
recently decorated, though some are
perhaps a little on the small side. There
is a pleasant terrace at the front for
when the British weather permits its
use. The basement restaurant is good
with a wide range of imaginative

dishes, especially for vegetarians. It is a little over-priced, though the wine list compensates. Last orders: 9.30pm.

Harrogate
🏠 ✕ 🚶 🐴 ☐ ££££
Old Swan Hotel, *Swan Road,*
Harrogate HG1 2SR
Tel: 0423-500055
Open all year; Library Restaurant closed
Sun, Wedgwood Room dinner only
This imposing ivy-covered hotel is the one Agatha Christie chose when she 'disappeared' in 1926. The rooms are not merely comfortable, they're luxurious. The feeling everywhere is one of space – from reception and lounges through to the bedrooms and bathrooms. The Library Restaurant has eye-catching stained glass windows, and an à la carte menu split into Preface, Manuscript and Epilogue. This tweeness also creeps into the names of the dishes, with a carousel of this, a gathering of that, but the food is superb. The Library Restaurant is open to non-residents, as is the separate fixed-price Wedgwood Room, an enormous and

elegant 200-seater. Last orders: Library Restaurant - lunch 2pm; dinner 10pm; Wedgwood Room - dinner 9.30pm.

Knaresborough
🏨 🚶 ☐ ££
The Yorkshire Lass, *High Bridge,*
Harrogate Road, Knaresborough HG5 8DA
Tel: 0423-862962
Open all year
A stunning display of flowers almost masks the front of this free house. Landlord Derek Speirs is Scottish and as well as real ales prides himself on his collection of fine malt whiskies. The six large bedrooms all have en suite bathrooms and old furniture that gives them a homely look. The lunch menu offers soup, sandwiches, pies and quiches, while the evening menu includes steak, chicken, duck, fresh fish, beef in ale and roast haunch of venison. One drawback if you like an early night might be the music three times a week, but that aside, the rooms are excellent value for money. Last orders: lunch 2.30pm; dinner 9.30pm (10pm in summer).

WHERE TO EAT

Harrogate
✕ ☐ £
Betty's, *Parliament Street, Harrogate*
Tel: 0423-502746
Open all year
You may queue to get in as there are no reservations and Betty's tea rooms are always busy. Once inside, you can have everything from a cup of tea to a four-course meal. Harrogate's favourite eating place seems to attract ladies who have just stepped out of a Beryl Cook painting: you put on weight merely looking at the cake trolley. With its views out over the gardens of the Stray, the upstairs room is popular, but

there's also a basement area. The menu is full of delights: Yorkshire fat rascals, Welsh rarebits in Theakston's ale and scrambled eggs with smoked salmon. The evening menu adds extra dishes, such as chicken Provençale and a Very Late Breakfast of sausage, egg, bacon, tomato and mushroom, though the wine list is limited to the Alsace region and is over-priced. Ten varieties of tea include such exotic delights as Yunnan Flowery Orange Pekoe, while coffee drinkers can choose from a dozen kinds of beans. All this and chocolate eclairs too. Open 9am-9pm.

Harrogate

× ▭ ££

Café Fleur, *3 Royal Parade, Harrogate*
Tel: 0423-503034
Open all year; dinner only
If you have only one meal in Harrogate, eat it here. Looking more like a smart café than a restaurant, this should appeal to anyone who enjoys eating out on the continent: superior food without snobbishness. The fixed-price menu has three courses, each with a choice of four dishes. There's an à la carte menu with daily specials such as lobster and dishes such as kebab of vegetables or salmon poached in herbs. For a very cheap meal the 'Petite Fleur' menu offers three courses of more limited choice. The fixed-price menus include a half-bottle of house wine, though you can choose a better wine from the extensive cellar and pay the difference. Service is efficient, friendly and unpretentious. Last orders 9.30pm.

Harrogate

× ▭ ££

William and Victoria's, *6 Cold Bath Road, Harrogate*
Tel: 0423-521510
Restaurant dinner only, closed Sun; wine bar closed Sat lunch and Sun
'Oh you must eat at William and Vic's,' a rival restaurant owner said, and it's easy to see why. There's a cosy cellar of a wine bar downstairs, with dim lights and privacy in quiet corners (reservations until 7.30pm only), and a more formal restaurant above, with a larger menu. The choice seems too large for everything to be freshly cooked, though that isn't noticeable when eating. Starters include smoked salmon, mari-

nated tuna with dill pickle and delicious baked mushrooms with bacon and basil. Main courses are reasonably priced: roast loin of Yorkshire lamb with fresh mint and hot garlic sauce, or sautéed pork fillet with wine, cream and spring onion sauce. The dessert menu has some pleasant surprises: mango, blackberry and sherry trifle, and a choice of six cheeses including an applewood smoked cheese. The wine list is as cheap and as wide-ranging as a wine bar's should be. Last orders: restaurant 10pm; wine bar lunch 2pm, dinner 10pm.

Wath-in-Nidderdale

  ▭ ££

The Sportsman's Arms, *Wath-in-Nidderdale, Pateley Bridge*
Tel: 0423-711306
Open all year; bar menu lunch only, restaurant dinner only, both closed Sun
The drive from Pateley Bridge to Wath is on a narrow, winding, country road, so watch for the sign for the Sportsman's Arms. This is an old sandstone coaching inn surrounded by trees, and falls somewhere between pub and restaurant. The food is superb, with fish a speciality. Fresh supplies arrive daily from Aberdeen, for daily specials like monkfish Provençal or poached haddock in a cheese sauce. The restaurant's fixed-price menu includes three courses, a half-bottle of house wine and coffee. The Sportsman's summer pudding is popular. Book ahead for the restaurant, but bar meals are available on a first-come first-served basis. Accommodation is available, in plainly furnished but comfortable country-style rooms. Last orders: bar 2pm, restaurant 9.30pm.

FROM RIPON TO RICHMOND

This is the low-lying country of Uredale and Bedale, mostly outside the National Park, but that's not to say that the scenery isn't beautiful. The approach to Richmond through Swaledale must be one of the most scenic drives in England, with wooded slopes tumbling down into the river valley. You could believe you were in Switzerland or Austria.

Possessing several good museums and a castle, Richmond is a town to visit in sunshine or showers. Ripon too is a mixture of indoor and outdoor activity with a cathedral, police museum, Thursday market and a lovely walk to nearby Fountains Abbey. Families can enjoy a day at the only amusement park in the Dales, Lightwater Valley, or visit Newby Hall, a country house with a miniature railway and adventure playground.

☆ CRAKEHALL WATER MILL

This is everyone's idea of a traditional flour mill, set in a pretty English village. The mill dates from the 17th century, and there has been one on this site at least since the Domesday Book was compiled. The machinery inside is from the 18th and 19th centuries, and though it was restored in 1980 it still creaks authentically when turned by the water of Crakehall Beck. The owner

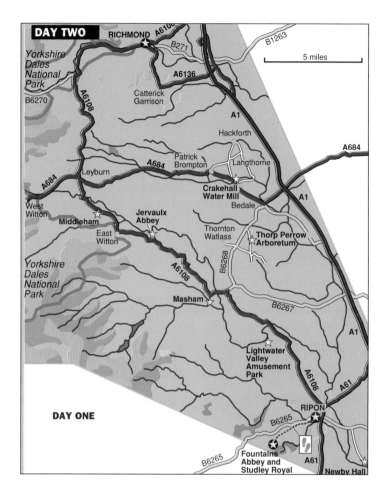

may show you round if he's not milling, or on summer week-ends when he employs extra staff, but it's basically a one-man operation. Milling usually takes place mid-week, although this is affected by water pressure and other variables, but the end result is flour made in exactly the same way that it has been for centuries. The mill now provides stone-ground wholemeal flour for many local restaurants, and sells to visitors.

Crakehall Mill, The Mill House, Little Crakehall, near Bedale. Tel: 0677-23240
Opening times: Easter-Sept - Sat, Sun, Tues-Thurs and Bank Hols 10am-5pm
Admission: adult 80p; child 50p

FOUNTAINS ABBEY AND STUDLEY ROYAL

The one unmissable feature in this corner of the Dales, even if you will have to share it with several hundred other visitors. For the most picturesque approach to the Abbey and Studley Royal Estate - on foot - from Ripon, see the Walk on p 30. The Abbey's new £2 million Visitors' Centre, opened in 1992, is sensitively concealed from the ruins, and provides many extra facilities. It incorporates a 200-seat restaurant, an auditorium which provides a continuous audio-visual display, and easier parking. Its spacious shop is the largest of any National Trust property, reflecting the fact that Fountains Abbey is its most visited attraction: over 300,000 visitors a year.

Enter through the Studley Royal gate. This allows you to walk through the impressive landscaped gardens which lead slowly round to a dramatic view of the Abbey's soaring ruins. In 1132, a group of dissident Benedictine monks from York arrived here, in what was a wilderness, and founded what became the richest Cistercian Abbey in mediaeval Britain. The ruins are in an excellent state of preservation, the nave as inspiring as any living cathedral, with its tall tower virtually intact. The whole site now has World Heritage status.

The Abbey buildings were the inspiration for the gardens in which they now stand. Created in the 18th century by John Aislabie, a former Chancellor of the Exchequer, these incorporate temples, ponds, a deer park, St Mary's Church, overgrown woods and the winding River Skell. To escape from the inevitable crowds, take some of the back paths up through the woods, particularly the one that leads to Anne Boleyn's Seat and which gives a stunning view down the river to the Abbey.

Free guided tours are available for both the Abbey and the Studley Royal Estate, leaving from the National Trust Visitors' Centre, and these are well recommended. There are snacks and drinks available, and it is a good idea to buy at least a basic guide to the grounds to make sure you don't miss some of the hidden buildings.

Fountains Abbey, Fountains, Ripon. Tel: 0765-620333
Opening times: daily 10am-dusk in winter except Dec 24/25 and certain Fris in Nov, Dec and Jan; Apr-June and Sept 10am-7pm, Jul and Aug 8pm. On Fri and Sat from Aug-Oct, the Abbey entrance stays open until 10.30pm and the Abbey is floodlit
Admission: adult £3.50; child £1.60 in summer; NT members free

Fountains Abbey   *Jervaulx Abbey*

JERVAULX ABBEY

In contrast to the tourist attraction of Fountains Abbey are the crumbling ruins of Jervaulx Abbey, where you may well be trusted to put your admission money in an honesty box, along with a few pence for a guide. This leaflet is vital as it transforms the heaps of old stones into a living, breathing Cistercian monastery once again – kitchens, monks' cells, chapels and drains can all be found on the ground plan. The name derives from the old name for Wensleydale - Yoredale - and the monks here were among the first to make the famous Wensleydale cheese. They also bred racehorses, a tradition continued today a few miles away in Middleham. Their idyllic-sounding life was brought to an end when the last abbot, Adam Sedburgh, was hanged at Tyburn Hill for taking part in a demonstration against the dissolution of the monasteries. The rural setting is beautiful and it's interesting to see both Fountains and Jervaulx, one pre-served, the other neglected. There's a small car park on the oppo-site side of the A6108 road, with a little café, children's play area and a crafts and plant shop. The Abbey is on private land, but with public access at any time, and if you go in the early morning or early evening you may well have the place to yourself.

Jervaulx Abbey, A6108, near Ripon
Opening times: daily, open access
Admission: adult £1; child 50p

LIGHTWATER VALLEY AMUSEMENT PARK

Completely hidden away in the Dales, the Park's 60 or so attractions include the biggest rollercoaster in the world and the largest 'pirate ship' in Britain, which swings passengers 60ft in the air. The admission cost may seem steep but it includes all the rides, all day. Ideas have been borrowed from the excellent American theme parks: litter patrols, a high staffing level and signs giving the current waiting time for each ride. You could consider leaving older children alone here and collecting them later in the day.

As for the rides, a favourite is the Rat. You enter by having to grope your way through a pitch-black tunnel with dripping walls and a whiff of the sewer about it. The ride itself – a fast rollercoaster in complete darkness – seemed to please most of the children who tried it, but compared to Disneyland's Space Mountain, the Rat is a mere gerbil. There are gentler rides like the Steam Train and Steam Boat for very young children, a go-kart track for the budding Nigel Mansell, a shooting gallery, pedal boats, BMX racers, bowling greens, putting, crazy golf, boules, a theatre, and plenty of gift shops and eating places. These range from burger bars to the more formal Farmyard Restaurant. Only a handful of the rides are closed if it's wet, and there's plenty to do under cover, like the dodgems, a hell slide, an underground river ride and the inevitable amusement arcade. But if it's likely to be your only visit, wait for a fine day... just don't let them drag you on to the rollercoaster.

Lightwater Valley Amusement Park, off the A6108, near Ripon. Tel: 0765-635368
Opening times: from 10am, closing time varies with season. Jul-Aug open daily; June
closed Mon and Tues ; May and Sept open weekends only; Oct open Sun only; Easter
open daily for two weeks. Dogs not allowed
Admission: £7.99; child under 4 free

☆ MASHAM

Masham is a small market town whose first market charter dates back to the 13th century, though sadly the market, held on Wednesday and Saturday, is only a small affair today. It's made all the smaller by the size of the vast cobbled square on which it's held, the square being the centre of town life – and the best place to park.

Masham has been home to **Theakston's Brewery**, housed in an old building near the Market Square, since 1827. No parking is allowed because of the drays, so walk and head for the Visitor Centre. Theakston's still provide beer to many pubs in the Dales, particularly their brew with the wonderful name and taste: Old Peculier. You'll discover that Peculier means particular, not peculiar, if you take one of the regular brewery tours, though you need to book ahead. If your guide happens to be Theakston's historian, John Todd, then you'll also learn a hundred more facts about the company, about Masham, brewing and anything and everything. He fires off information like Ken Dodd cracks jokes.

The day tours, which involve climbing narrow steep stairs, take place while the brewery is working, so be prepared for the noise, heat and smells of brewing. The evening tours are more peaceful but generally limited to organised parties, with a few individuals accepted if there's room. It's then that you can see the coopers at work: one-fifth of Britain's coopers work at Theakston's, all two of them - Clive and Alastair. Clive has a dry delivery and a fund of stories, and he may help organise a build-a-barrel competition afterwards. Theakston's must be the only brewery in the country to have an artist-in-residence. John Blakey was originally commissioned to paint a portrait of Clive, which when finished will be on display in the Visitor Centre, but this local artist has gone on to paint and sketch other scenes of brewery life. The Visitor Centre is small and well arranged, with displays of pub games and Theakston's history, but is hardly worth visiting on its own. It is also, paradoxically, unable to serve beer at lunchtime!

The Brewery, Masham, near Ripon, North Yorkshire HG4 4DX. Tel: 0765-689057 Ext. 4317

Opening times: tours daily at noon and 4pm, must be pre-booked. Visitor Centre: 10.30am-4pm (closed for lunch 1-2pm); Good Fri-Oct 31, Wednes-Sun; Nov-mid Dec, Wednes, Sat and Sun only. Closed mid Dec-Maundy Thurs

Admission: tour - adult £2.50; child 10-18 £2; Visitor Centre - adult £1; child 50p

Glass-blowing at Uredale Glass, Masham

Masham has attracted a trio of interesting craft workers. The craft workshops are all within a few yards of each other, down a mews alley behind the King's Head Hotel on Market Square. Each workshop has a shop attached, and the crafts on display are of such good and varied quality that time ought to be found for a visit.

At the **Masham Pottery** (0765-89762) you can sometimes see potter Howard Charles throwing clay on the wheel or putting spouts on teapots, and he's always happy to explain his craft to visitors.

Next door is **Handmade Jewellery**, the hands belonging to Delyth St John Lewis, Jorvik Young Craftsperson of the Year in 1989. She specialises in finely-wrought original designs in both precious and non-precious metals: rings, necklaces, ear-rings. It is fascinating to watch as she coaxes metals into curves or etches on a design, but she may be away buying, selling or exhibiting. The shop will still be open, however.

Across the yard, **Uredale Glass** (0765-89780) gives a rare chance to see glass being blown, coloured and shaped. A small charge is made for the demonstrations, which take place throughout the day. It is intriguing to see the glass being handled in its various states, especially when spun out finely into the neck of a swan, as glassmakers Tim and Maureen Simon demonstrate their skills; the accompanying talk is informative. A large gift shop offers a wide selection of glassware.

☆ MIDDLEHAM

There is not much to *do* in Middleham, the smallest town in Yorkshire, but it's a lovely place on a hill with a large cobbled square. There are over a dozen racing stables in the vicinity and if you are staying here you will hear the clatter of hooves on cobbles as the horses go for their morning exercise. You can follow them and watch as they go through their paces on the Gallops, a stretch of open grassland above the town. It's a thrilling sight in the chill morning air, and well worth getting up early for.

Middleham Castle, standing slightly above the town, is a well-preserved and atmospheric ruin. The central keep dates back to the 12th century, and during the Wars of the Roses Edward IV and Henry VI were both imprisoned here. Its closest connection is with Richard III, who trained here as a Knight and whose son Edward is said to have been born in what is now the Prince's Tower. A modern claim to fame is the discovery of the 15th-century Middleham Jewel, a magnificent gold pendant containing a sapphire valued at £2.5 million, though only a replica is on display here as the original is in the Yorkshire Museum in York. Another £1 million piece of jewellery was also found by the roadside – making a visit to Middleham look more attractive all the time.

Middleham Castle, Middleham. Tel: 0969-23899
Opening times: daily Good Fri or Apr 1 (whichever is earlier)-Sept 30, 10am-6pm; in winter Tues-Sun 10am-4pm
Admission: adult £0.95; child 5-18 45p

River Ure near Middleham

Middleham Castle

☆ NEWBY HALL

The English stately home in all its glory, complete with modern entertainments such as a miniature railway, adventure playground, picnic area, even an exercise area for dogs – plus the acres of car parking that are needed to cope with the visitors. The business-like approach ensures that everything runs smoothly. The licensed self-service restaurant offers a decent choice of basic meals and snacks, there's a well-stocked shop, plants for sale, and a good selection of cheap leaflets covering various aspects of the house and gardens.

In the grounds a woodland discovery walk takes you through pine trees and an orchard down to the banks of the River Ure, where you might be lucky and see one of the kingfishers. Around the Hall are more formal gardens, enjoyable whatever the season and including rose gardens, pergolas, rock gardens and water gardens.

The estate dates back to at least the 13th century, and in 1697 Newby Hall was described by Celia Fiennes in her travel journal as 'the finest house I saw in Yorkshire'. Wings have been added, changes made, and most of the interior - remodelled by Robert Adam - dates from the 18th century, but it remains a magnificent building. The Tapestry Room is wonderful, its walls covered in the most delicate of dove-grey Gobelins tapestries, with tapestried Chippendale chairs, too.

Another visitor was Charlotte Brontë, in 1839, who heard the local legend which said that a madwoman had been confined in an attic at Newby Hall in the 18th century. This tale may well have inspired the similar fate which befell the first Mrs Rochester in *Jane Eyre*.

An amusing attraction is the Chamber Pot Room, where faces leer up from the bottom of some of the pots, and ribald messages are printed round the rims of others. You are free to wander round at your own pace. Guides are on hand in all the rooms to answer any questions. Newby Hall is unashamedly touristy, and popular with coach parties – because it's a good day out.

Newby Hall, near Skelton, off B6265, Ripon. Tel: 0423-322583
Opening times: Mar 28-Sept 29, daily except Mon: gardens and restaurant open 11am; house and railway open at noon. Last entry: house 4.30pm, gardens 5pm
Admission: £4.50 a car for house and gardens

RICHMOND

Richmond has one of the most attractive settings in Yorkshire, with its castle towering over the River Swale, its large market square and some very steep cobbled streets. You almost need mountain gear to get from the river to the castle. There isn't that much to do when you reach **Richmond Castle**, other than wander round and climb up the battlements, but despite that it's something to be seen, with grand views over the river from the top of the 100ft keep. There's also a lovely view down on to the market square, or to nearby Easby Abbey and the Culloden Tower on the edge of the town. There are several enormous but empty rooms to explore, and children seem to be able to amuse themselves in these, looking through the windows and running up and down the narrow stairways.

Richmond Castle. Tel: 0748-822493
Opening times: Good Fri or Apr 1 (whichever is earlier)-Sept 30, daily 10am-6pm;
otherwise Tues-Sun 10am-4pm
Admission: adult 50p; child 30p

(i) Richmond **Tourist Information Centre** is at Friary Gardens in Victoria Road; tel: 0748-850252.

Richmond Theatre Museum is the best of Richmond's three museums. This is thanks to the lively tours provided free at regular intervals throughout the day by the volunteer guides, who really bring the theatre to life. It is the only Georgian theatre in the world that survives in its original state, having been built in 1788 by actor-manager Samuel Butler. It then seated 400 people, a seat in the gallery costing one shilling. Down below, the stalls seats are rows of pew-like benches, and the stage itself is as deep as it is wide, almost like a child's toy theatre. The original box office and cramped stairways can still be seen. The atmosphere is haunting. There are old playbills on display and photographs of visiting stars and royals, but the real star is the theatre itself. Shows are still performed three times a week between March and December. They range from classic plays and one-man shows to opera and ballet performances.

Richmond Theatre Museum, Victoria Road, Richmond. Tel: 0748-823021 (2.30-5pm)
Opening times: daily Easter-Oct 31, 11am-4.45pm (Sun opens 2.30pm)
Admission: adult £1; child 70p

The Green Howards Museum is a fine example of a modern museum – bright, well-displayed and thorough – but it must be said that it is mainly for the military enthusiast. It contains 300 years of the history of the famous North Yorkshire Regiment, with 80 uniforms, 3,000 medals and other decorations, campaign relics from the Crimea to the Falklands, paintings and drawings, buttons and badges, regimental colours, a 17th-century musket and the blood-stained pistol holsters of the Grand Old Duke of York himself. If you want to know whether he really did have 10,000 men, this is the place to come because he served in the Green Howards.

The Green Howards Museum, Trinity Church Square, Richmond. Tel: 0748-822133
Opening times: Apr-Oct daily 9.30am-4.30pm (Sun opens 2pm); Mar and Nov closed
Sun; Feb open Mon-Fri 10am-4.30pm; Dec and Jan closed
Admission: adult £1; child 50p

The **Richmond Museum** itself is not one of the best museums in the Dales, or even in Richmond. Its main exhibit is the surgery set from the first television series of *All Creatures Great and Small*. It was purchased from the BBC after the first series, and when they decided to do a second they asked for it back, but the museum refused and so the BBC had to build another. That apart, the museum has only a small collection of local items, lacking the bizarre and unexpected gems that bring other museums in the area to life.

Richmond Museum, Ryder's Wynd, Richmond. Tel: 0748-825611
Opening times: daily Mar 29-Nov 2, 11am-5pm
Admission: adult 50p; child 30p

★ RIPON

Ripon has much to recommend it, especially on its Thursday market day, but the star turn is **Ripon Cathedral**. The most striking feature of this magnificent building is the Crypt of St Wilfred, dating back to 672 and the oldest crypt in any English cathedral. Walking along the narrow 45ft passage that leads down into the dark, bare chamber is so eery it's like entering your own tomb. Some fine stained glass dates from the 13th century, and take care not to miss the strange and sometimes grotesque carvings found under the hinged seats in the choir stalls, which are 500 years old. The small shop is well-stocked with a range of guides and it's worth buying one of them, at least, so that you know what you're looking at.

(i) The Ripon **Tourist Office** is across the road from the Cathedral entrance, at Minster Road; tel: 0765-604625.

On **market day**, be sure to be there for 11am when the market is officially opened (several hours after it actually starts) by the Ripon Bellringer, who stands opposite the Town Hall and will be finished before the unwary even know that he's there. Also worth noting in the Market Place – hard to miss at 90ft tall – is the 200-year-old obelisk, designed by the famous architect, Nicholas Hawksmoor. If you are here in the evening, watch for the Ripon Hornblower, who blows his horn at the four corners of the obelisk at exactly 9pm. This dates back to the announcement of the setting of the watch, when the safety of the city was put into the hands of the wakeman (now the mayor) and his constables. Any householder robbed after the horn was blown was entitled to claim compensation from the wakeman.

Ripon Cathedral

The unusual **Ripon Police Museum** is worth finding. Housed on two floors in what was once the cell block of Ripon Prison (and it looks it), this museum is just the thing if you've ever wanted to see the history of handcuffs, police bicycles or truncheons. Children will love it – stocks, prison cells, gallows, a display on how to investigate a murder. Nothing to put you off your lunch, but still gruesome enough to be interesting. On the more serious side, it tells a good tale of the development of law and order, and of the police force from its origins in the 18th century.

Ripon Police Museum, St Marygate, Ripon. Tel: 0765-690799
Opening times: Easter-Oct Mon-Fri and Sun 1-5pm; Jul and Aug only, weekday opening time 11am. Closed Sat
Admission: adult 80p; child 40p

FROM RIPON TO FOUNTAINS ABBEY

There is a much better way to reach the twin attractions of Studley Royal and Fountains Abbey than by merely turning up in the car park. Instead, leave your car in Ripon and walk out along the B6265 road, marked Pateley Bridge. You pass the Spa Baths on your left, then cross Bishopton Bridge. A few hundred yards beyond the bridge, at the end of a wood on the left, a sign indicates the path to take across the fields towards Studley Roger. Follow the footpath into fields full of wheat which, at the right time of year, are dotted with vivid red poppies and full of the sounds of yellowhammers. The path is fairly well-trodden and easy to follow.

In Studley Roger you emerge between a couple of houses, and go straight across the main road where the path picks up again, with a farm on your left-hand side. After passing through a field you will see the gate which marks the entrance into the Studley Royal Estate. From here any dogs must be on a lead, because as soon as you pass through the gate – perhaps only 30 minutes after leaving Ripon – you should see the first of the Studley Royal herds of deer. There are about 300 deer in all, mostly fallow deer but you may also see the larger Sika deer and the even larger red deer. They tend to stay well away from the road so that people arriving by car may not even be aware of them, but on foot you may be able to get up quite close, if you move very slowly so as not to startle them. When you are ready to look round the Studley Royal gardens proper, head to the left which brings you to the main entrance road. To return, simply retrace your steps.

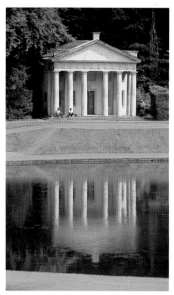

Studley Royal Estate – Temple of Piety and Sweet (or Spanish) Chestnut

☆ THORP PERROW ARBORETUM

A short drive from Thornton Watlass, this is an essential stop for keen gardeners to make. The collection was begun by Sir Leonard Ropner in 1927, after his father gave him 65 acres of parkland, where some of the original oaks date back to the time of Henry VIII. Sir Leonard's enthusiasm took him all over the world collecting tree and plant specimens, which are displayed in so natural a way that the garden gives the impression of wild woodland, crossed by wide grassy paths. It's all well-labelled and organised, though. Now owned by Sir John and Lady Ropner, the arboretum contains over 2,000 species of trees and shrubs: ancient oaks, Japanese maples, a varnish tree, over 60 varieties of lilac. The paths are signposted clearly but unobtrusively, and the species discreetly labelled or numbered, but it's worth investing in the basic map and leaflet to ensure you don't miss anything. Enthusiasts can also buy a more comprehensive booklet which describes the collection and tells you where to find everything. Light snacks and drinks may be available at the entrance, from the van which also sells the tickets, and there's a picnic area. Even on a hot Saturday afternoon in mid-summer it is possible to walk alone in the grounds and admire the collection of trees – or simply sit and read, or soak up the sun.

Thorp Perrow Arboretum, Bedale. Tel: 0677-25323
Opening times: dawn until dusk, all year
Admission: adult £1.50; child £1

Thorp Perrow Arboretum, Bedale

The Buck Inn at Thornton Watlass, pleasantly situated on the green of this picturesque village, serves excellent food. The lunch menu includes home-made soup, steak and kidney pie, deep-fried fresh Whitby cod, home-cooked ham, salmon mousse, baked aubergines. In the evenings the menu expands to include beefsteak braised in ale, grilled fresh salmon steak in parsley butter or pork fillet in creamed mushrooms. The beer is as good as the food: Theakston's, Tetley's and John Smith's, all served from the cask. Food served every day, from noon-2pm and 6.45-9.30pm.

WHERE TO STAY

Crakehall

♿ ⅋8 ✉ ££

Blairgowrie Guesthouse, *near Crakehall, Bedale, N Yorks DL8 1JZ*
Tel: 0748-811377
Open Easter-end Oct

'We've only ever had one complaint about Mrs Knox,' said the Bedale tourist office, 'and that's that she overfeeds people. They say you can get all day on one of her breakfasts.' Well, you may need an evening meal, which Mrs Knox can also provide. There are only two spacious double bedrooms, each with their own bathrooms, neatly furnished in a homely country style. Mr Knox has retired from farming and the rambling old stone farmhouse was recently modernised. It stands alone at the end of an open approach road, commanding lovely views of rolling fields full of sheep.

Jervaulx

🏠 ⅋⅋ ✉ ✉ £££

Jervaulx Hall Country House Hotel, *Jervaulx, Ripon, N Yorks HG4 4PH*
Tel: 0677-60235
Open Feb-Nov

A beautiful Victorian stone ivy-covered house surrounded by trees, shrubs and flowers, Jervaulx Hall is next to the ruins of Jervaulx Abbey. The owners encourage a friendly country house atmosphere, and bookings must include dinner: good simple home cooking using the best cuts of meat. This arrangement may not be to everyone's taste but Jervaulx Hall is a wonderful place to indulge yourself if it is. The owners are brisk and jolly, full of ideas for things to do and showing great concern that every aspect of your stay

should be perfect. There are five twin and five double rooms, all huge, bright and decorated to the highest standards.

Masham

♿ ⅋5 ✉ ✉ ££

Bank Villa, *Masham, Ripon, N Yorks HG4 4DB*
Tel: 0765-689605
Open Easter-Oct

A small Georgian stone house on the edge of Masham with views of the River Ure and set back from the A6108, Bank Villa has an air of comfortable gentility. Interesting collections of books abound, the owners are charming and the house manages to retain its Georgian atmosphere without forsaking modern conveniences. The food is a highlight, Phillip Gill being a noted cook, and much of the produce comes from their own kitchen garden – where there's also a summerhouse for guests. The seven bedrooms all have washbasins and four have showers, but toilets are shared. There are also two lounges, one with a television.

Middleham

♿ ⅋⅋ ✉ ✉ ££

Greystones, *Market Place, Middleham, N Yorks DL8 4NR*
Tel: 0969-22016
Open all year

A very comfortable and smart Georgian house overlooking Middleham's Market Place, where the only interruption to your sleep will be the early morning clip-clop of horses' hooves on the cobblestones beneath the front windows: there are several stables nearby. The four rooms are all a good size with en suite shower and toilet. They are very tastefully decorated, and guests also have the use of a TV lounge with an open log fire. There's a lovely homely feel about Greystones, with dinner available if required. The enterprising owners also offer special activity weekends such as bird watching, yoga, cookery, walking, flower arranging.

Middleham
🏠 ✕ ▭ £££

The Miller's House Hotel, *Market Place, Middleham, N Yorks DL8 4NR*
Tel: 0969-22630
Open all year; R dinner only
This grey-stone Grade II listed building, dating from 1726, is set back slightly from Middleham's Market Place in its own quiet yard. There are eight bright and comfortable bedrooms, including a glorious four-poster room with a Victorian roll-top bath. The owners, Judith and Crossley Sutherland, do genuinely care about your comfort in what must be one of the best hotels for miles. Its restaurant is open to non-residents. The choices are pleasingly different on the fixed-price three-course menu. Starters might include borek (a Greek dish comprising feta cheese in filo pastry and served with tomato sauce), while the main courses may be chicken Simla or quenelles of halibut. Wide choice of puddings – or no choice if the chocolate rum pot is on the menu, which has so much alcohol it ought to be restricted to non-drivers. Last orders: 9.30pm.

Ripon
🗑 👫 📪 £££

The Nordale Private Hotel, *1-2 North Parade, North Road, Ripon, N Yorks HG4 1ES*
Tel: 0765-603557
Open all year

A substantial Victorian house looking out over Ripon's main North Road, it is set far enough back for guests not to be too disturbed by the noise. The house is airy and comfortable, and most rooms have en suite bathrooms or shower cubicles, although some are cramped into corners. The low rates, however, reflect this, and are very reasonable for a place that's ideal for both Ripon and a quick getaway to the surrounding countryside. The owners are extremely hospitable in typical Yorkshire fashion, providing an evening meal if required. Large private car park, a bonus in Ripon.

Thornton Watlass
📭 👫 🛏 ▭ £££

The Buck Inn, *Thornton Watlass, near Bedale, Ripon, N Yorks HG4 4AH*
Tel: 0677-422461
Open all year
With an ideal setting on the edge of the green of this beautiful village, The Buck Inn has only one drawback for guests – moving your car from the front of the pub when there's a cricket match, as the pub wall is part of the boundary. If you don't want to relax in the bar itself with its open fire, there's a residents' lounge with TV and a play area for children. There are five rooms (one family, one single, three twin/double), all with private bath or shower. Plainly decorated but clean and modern, they offer good value. The Buck Inn also has an excellent reputation for food, with picnic lunches available for residents. The landlord, Michael Fox, is quiet and unassuming, very polite and helpful, and with his wife Margaret runs the ideal British pub.

WHERE TO EAT

Masham
✕ ▭ ££

The Floodlite, *7 Silver Street,*
Masham
Tel: 0765-89000
Closed Mon-Thurs lunch, Mon dinner
With a wonderful welcome you are
led to a French-style bar in the basement to have a drink and give the
menu the attention it deserves. The
dining room is at street level and its
only drawback is the absence of cur-
tains to prevent passers-by from
examining the contents of your plate.
So when booking ask for a table away
from the window. The Floodlite's fine
English cooking includes game spe-
cialities. Delicious hot home-made
wholemeal rolls, starters such as hare
and pistachio nut pâté in a blackcur-
rant sauce or salmon and pike terrine
with lobster sauce, then a generous
helping of rack of lamb or roast loin
of venison. Puddings include apple
and almond flan and blackberry and
apple bread and butter pudding.
Easily the best food in the area. Last
orders: lunch 2pm; dinner 9.30pm.

Ripon
⌘ ▭ ££

The Old Deanery, *Minster Road,*
Ripon
Tel: 0765-603518
Open daily
The Old Deanery is a fine old house,
once home to the Deans of Ripon. Its
restaurant is fittingly old-fashioned
in style, though there's nothing old-
fashioned about the cooking. The
lunch menu may include a tasty
venison pie and Berner Rösti (grated
potato, bacon and shallots fried in a
cake and served with a salad). The

fixed-price evening menu puts the
emphasis on fish, for example salmon
in a lattice pastry parcel with mint,
chives and a herb sauce, or poached
fillet of turbot with a prawn and
mussel sauce. Puddings include the
intriguing Eton mess, a concoction of
strawberries, cream, meringue and a
raspberry sauce. Graham and
Daphne Dooley also have two guest-
rooms, and it's worth booking ahead
in order to get one. Both are huge
doubles, and the bathroom in the rear
room is larger than most hotel rooms,
while the front room looks out on
Ripon Cathedral. Last orders: lunch
2pm; dinner 10pm.

West Witton
🏠 ▭ £££

The Wensleydale Heifer, *West*
Witton, Leyburn
Tel: 0969-22322
Open daily
There's a small bistro at the front of
this 17th-century inn, and you can
also eat in the bar from the bistro
menu, which includes mainly fish but
also steaks, pies and a couple of vegetarian dishes too. The food is acceptable if predictable. The rear restaurant with its well-spaced candle-lit
tables has a better reputation. The
dinner menu offers a wide choice
with an emphasis on steak and fish:
fresh mussels, langoustines or
prawns à la pil pil, followed by
salmon, halibut or Swaledale rain-
bow trout. It's good to see wines recommended for each dish, from a
large and affordable list. There are
also 19 country-style bedrooms, some
with four-posters, all well-equipped
and smart. Last orders: lunch 2pm;
dinner 9.30pm.

THE HEART OF THE DALES

Wensleydale is the best known of the Dales, and though it runs for over 40 miles until it leaves the Dales beyond Ripon, here around Hawes and Askrigg it is at its best. Grand in scale yet gentle in its contours, with dry-stone walls and sweeping green fields, it is filled with the familiar sight of flocks of Wensleydale sheep. Rainfall is high here so come prepared, and bear in mind that if it's wet in one place, it's quite possibly sunny and dry ten miles down the road.

The rainfall does make some attractions more impressive, and the ideal time to see these is in sunshine after a heavy downpour. There's the triple-decker Aysgarth Falls, Hardrow Force - the highest waterfall in England, and the natural expanse of Semer Water. For a family day out visit Bolton Castle and the museum at Reeth, then spend a few hours in Hawes, with its museum, ropemakers, gallery, shops and bustling weekly livestock market.

There's a lovely drive around the various villages featured in James Herriot's *All Creatures Great and Small*, and no one should miss West Burton, one of the most beautiful villages in the country. This, though, is really a region for those who enjoy striding out in the fresh air, and the Askrigg Waterfalls Walk will help you do just that.

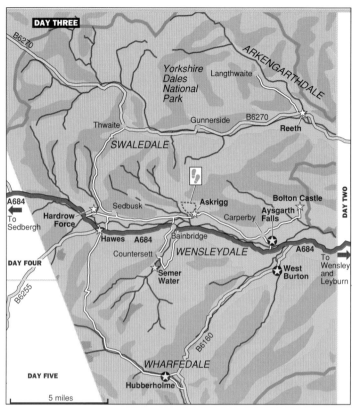

DAY THREE

B6270

Yorkshire
Dales
National
Park

Langthwaite

ARKENGARTHDALE

Thwaite

Gunnerside

B6270

Reeth

SWALEDALE

A684

To
Sedbergh

Hardrow
Force

Sedbusk

Askrigg

Bolton Castle

Aysgarth
Falls

Carperby

Hawes A684

Bainbridge

DAY TWO

Countersett

WENSLEYDALE

A684

To
Wensley
and
Leyburn

DAY FOUR

B6255

Semer
Water

West
Burton

DAY FIVE

B6160

WHARFEDALE

Hubberholme

5 miles

☆ ASKRIGG

Askrigg is a small village of Dales stone houses dating back to
pre-Norman times and is attractive yet rugged. Its fame has
increased since the BBC chose it for filming *All Creatures Great
and Small*, the television series based on James Herriot's vet
books (see p 44). While it can become crowded with sightseers
in summer, the village makes few concessions to tourism.

The **Askrigg Woodturners** are not a trade union or a folk
group, but two separate shops that happen to be in the same
village. Ivor Grace and John Stirling are both happy for visitors
to watch them work, and both offer a similar selection of finely
crafted wooden items for sale, from tiny objects such as light-
pulls to bowls, lamps, barometers, sticks and stools. 'Some of

my export orders come from Africa,' says Ivor Grace, 'which is quite funny as that's where a lot of my wood comes from in the first place, so they send it several thousand miles to Yorkshire, then I turn it and send it back again.' Ivor Grace is on Elm Hill (tel: 0969-50663), and John Stirling at Grenada, opposite the Crown Inn (tel: 0969-50334). Both are open daily in summer and on weekdays in winter, 9am-5.30pm.

ASKRIGG WATERFALLS WALK

Askrigg is a very pleasant village, but having found the Herriot connections the visitor might want a little more from a visit, and this easy and varied walk of a couple of hours provides just that. From the Askrigg Market Cross outside the church, walk down the road to the right of the church and pick up the footpath signs marked Mill Gill Force. This is the first of two waterfalls you reach, after crossing a few fields and walking through the woods. The path is well signposted. From Mill Gill, walk back to the path you were on and turn right, keeping close to the wall. You soon pick up the next signpost, for Whitfield Gill, and to reach this simply head upstream, though views of the Gill are disappointingly distant. Carry on up the woodland path, over a stile and turn right onto a farm track, which is Low Straits Lane. This eventually takes you back onto the road into Askrigg, where you turn right, walking back down into the village, past the shop of Ivor Grace, the woodturner.

✪ AYSGARTH FALLS

A few miles from Askrigg is one of the region's biggest attractions, the Aysgarth Falls. These are impressive for their width, not their height, and for the fact that there are three separate sets of falls on the same river, the Ure. At one time Wensleydale was called Uredale. The falls are well sign-posted, and invariably busy, so an early or late visit is recommended. To view them you need to park at the **Dales National Park Centre**, where you would be advised to pay the all-day parking charge, rather than the one-hour alternative, as that is not long enough to take in the falls and the nearby gift shops, the good tea shop and the Vintage Carriage Museum. From the car park, the short walk to the upper falls and the slightly longer one to the middle and

lower falls are both clearly marked. A small charge for viewing
the upper falls has recently been introduced, but if you object to
that then cross over the river by the bridge outside the car park
and there's a more distant view from the road. At the time of
writing you could still enjoy the middle and lower falls for free.

The **Mill Race Teashop** near the bridge just below the Upper
Falls has an excellent range of salads and snacks, with home-
made cakes and a few hot meals such as sausage pie. It was in
these buildings around the bridge, formerly called Yore Mill,
that the shirts for Garibaldi's army were made.

Aysgarth Falls

The former mill buildings also contain the **Vintage Carriage
Museum**, a delightful and interesting collection of all kinds of
vehicle. Broughams and landaus, which sound like a music hall
act, are here, along with penny-farthings, sleighs, Irish jaunting

39

cars and Welsh hearses. There are short descriptions of most of
the vehicles, enough to help you conjure up a picture of them in
use: 'This landau carried the Lord Mayor of Manchester to the
Royal Lancashire Show in 1904'. Can't you just see him sitting
upright in his regalia? There's a tub trap, a cosy car, a fire engine
called Albert and an American buggy last used by a student at
Cambridge University in about 1930. There's even a haunted cab.

Vintage Carriage Museum, Aysgarth Falls, Leyburn
Opening times: Easter-Oct, weekdays 11am-5pm, Bank Hols and weekends 11am-6pm
Admission: adult £1.50; child 50p

☆ ## BOLTON CASTLE

Castle Bolton is the name of the village, north of Aysgarth, and
Bolton Castle the small castle you'll find when you get there.
Built in the late 14th century, and destroyed in 1647 following
the Civil War, it then remained empty for 300 years. Its present
owner, the Hon. Harry Orde-Powlett, therefore earns full marks
for trying to do something different and give these castle
remains an authentically austere atmosphere: the lighting is dim,
the furnishings limited, the rooms look exceedingly uncomfort-
able to live in. Shadows in the corners sometimes conceal figures,
only revealed when your eyes get used to the light. A very effec-
tive dungeon might give you a fright, and remind you what conditions were like. An arm-bone was found in the dungeon, still
bearing its heavy manacle, the prisoners being chained to the
rock visible in one corner of this nasty hole in the ground.
Elsewhere you begin to hear some chanting, so slight that you
wonder if you've imagined it. Follow the sound and you find a
monk's cell, just off the chapel. The lack of signposting encour-
ages you to be adventurous and seek out the surprises. One bed-
chamber is thought to be where Mary Queen of Scots was
imprisoned for several months in 1568. The view from the top of
the remaining battlements is not for those who suffer from verti-
go. They might prefer to wander back to the shop and snack bar
for a cup of tea and a scone. A guidebook is available and useful
to have.

Bolton Castle, Castle Bolton, near Leyburn. Tel: 0969-23981
Opening times: daily Mar-mid Nov, 10am-5pm
Admission: adult £2; child £1

Bolton Castle

Hardrow Force

☆ HARDROW FORCE

The waterfall at Hardrow has two claims to distinction. First, it has the longest straight drop of any waterfall in England – 100ft. Second, it must be the only waterfall in the country that you have to pass through a pub to visit. The pub, the Green Dragon, is open from 11am-11pm so there's almost permanent access. Many guidebooks refer to the fall as Hardraw Force, but the village it's named after is Hardrow, a tiny agricultural gathering of houses and farms. Parking is a problem on the narrow road so you should be sensible and contribute to the official parking scheme, or the unofficial ones when farmers open their fields for use. Pass through the pub, pausing only to pay your few pence at the bar, and walk past the toilets, out of the back, and half a mile or so along the path that leads through some trees and stops at the amphitheatre where, once a year, a brass band concert is held. All year round, except when it's frozen in winter, the water of Fossdale Beck plunges over a rock-face into a pool beneath.

Many people ignore the warnings to stay clear and walk round behind the falls, although it's only a narrow chute of water so the thrill of it hardly seems worth the risk of slipping on wet rocks.

☆ HAWES

Hawes is the main market town in this part of the Dales, a bustling place, especially on Tuesday when market stalls line either side of the main street. More interesting by far is the **Livestock Market**, also held every Tuesday morning at the auction rooms, a minute's walk along the main A684 road towards Leyburn. Do go, it makes you realise that farm life in the Dales is alive and well, not merely a museum piece. Auctions are open to anyone, of course, so wander around but try not to wave at the wrong moment or you may find yourself owning a flock of sheep. Most of the animal pens are inside, as is the auction itself, so it's a good place to go on a wet day, full of atmosphere and farmers' gossip.

The **Dales Countryside Museum** is housed in the old station yard, and is more modern and organised than most rural museums. It perhaps lacks a little of the amateur haphazardness that makes others appealing, but it has a comprehensive collection of mainly farming exhibits: cheese- and butter-making, sheep-farming and peat-cutting. There's a 400 million-year-old piece of Wensleydale granite, and a fascinating display on the hand-knitting industry which flourished here and in nearby Dent until the turn of the century. Another attraction is the section on local craftsmen, covering carpenters, cobblers, blacksmiths, stick makers and others.

The same building houses the combined **Hawes Tourist Information and National Park Centres**, with a very good range of books, postcards and leaflets detailing walks. When the office is closed there is still a 24-hour Teletext information service by the door, covering accommodation and local attractions.

Dales Countryside Museum, Station Yard, Hawes. Tel: 0969-667450
Opening times: daily Apr-Oct, 10am-5pm (last admission 4.30pm) and some winter weekends
Admission: adult £1; child 50p

Outside Station Yard is **Hawes Ropemakers**, a combined factory and shop where, on our visit, a half-hearted display of rope-making was going on. We are assured by locals, however, that this is not normally the case, so we suggest you pay a visit. The shop sells a good range of rope products: dog leads, washing lines, skipping ropes.

The **Wensleydale Gallery** (tel: 0969-667661) sells paintings, photographs, postcards, pottery and general country knick-knackery. There are no frills about this place – bare brick walls and trestle tables – and an air of the jumble sale about it, but in among the tat there are some good paintings to be found. Open daily from 10.30am-5.30pm, between Easter and the end of October, although it may be closed on some Wednesday afternoons in early summer.

Anyone wanting a book on the Dales should try **Kit Calvert's Secondhand Bookshop**, which is 'up t'ginnel' on Market Place (tel: 0969-667667). If you don't know what a ginnel is, perhaps one of Kit Calvert's books on Yorkshire dialect might help you discover that a ginnel is a back alley. In addition to Dales and dialect, the shop specialises in poetry and books by Hilaire Belloc and G K Chesterton. There are also shelves full of cheap paperbacks.

The shop is of interest because of its former owner, Kit Calvert himself, who was also very much involved in the local Wensleydale cheese industry. The first Wensleydale factory was on the edge of Hawes, at Gayle Beck, and when it was on the verge of bankruptcy Kit Calvert rescued it and reversed its fortunes by suggesting it should market the small, one-pound, round Wensleydale cheeses that you will still find in local shops. Earlier Calvert had formed a delegation of local farmers to petition the Ministry of Agriculture when proposed legislation in the 1940s threatened the centuries-old Wensleydale recipe. Thankfully they succeeded, although it's a pity that visitors can no longer see the Wensleydale cheese being made in the handful of remaining factories. The Bookshop opens April-September - Monday-Saturday 10am-5pm, Sunday 2-5pm; October-March - Tuesday, Saturday and Sunday afternoon.

THE HERRIOT CONNECTION

James Herriot's tales of life as a Yorkshire vet in the 1930s and 1940s, and their later television and film adaptations, bring hundreds of thousands of visitors to the Yorkshire Dales every year. The fact that Herriot himself originally came from Glasgow, and his veterinary practice wasn't in the Dales at all, doesn't seem to matter. The town where he worked was Thirsk, to the east of the Dales, referred to in the books as Darrowby. When the series came to be filmed, Thirsk wasn't considered right for the period, and the settings were shifted into the Dales, where fewer changes needed making to create the authentic rural look.

Askrigg was chosen to represent Darrowby, and the cast and crew normally stayed at the King's Arms Hotel there. The back bar of the hotel was also used for filming, as the Drover's Arms, no doubt because it looks as if it hasn't changed since the 1830s, let alone the 1930s. Near the Market Cross in Askrigg is Cringley House, a tall building with iron railings which was used for exterior shots of Herriot's Skeldale House.

Carperby features in both the real life and fictional Herriot worlds. The village hall was used for shooting a village dance, while the author and his wife spent their honeymoon at the Wheatsheaf. Close by is Castle Bolton, where James Herriot proposed to Helen – on television, that is.

Hawes was used for filming scenes of the Darrowby Cattle Mart, which were shot in Hawes' own livestock market that is held every Tuesday. To the north of Hawes is **Hardrow,** where the Parish Church has been used to represent Darrowby Church, and north of Hardrow is **Simonstone Hall**, scene of the Country Club and Darrowby Show.

Reeth has also been used to represent parts of Darrowby, principally Langhorn House which was used as Skeldale House in the film *It Shouldn't Happen to a Vet*. The Buck Inn and several local shops have been seen in the various television series. In fact if you take the road marked Arkengarthdale alongside the Buck Inn and drive three miles to **Langthwaite,** you will see on your right the bridge over Arkle Beck which was used in the opening credits of the television series. If you then take the left turn towards Low Row, you will be able to drive through the very same water splash that is also a feature of the opening sequence.

Wensley has a lovely old church which was built in 1245 and provided the setting for the wedding of Herriot and his wife, Helen. These are the best-known places used, but of course filming took place all over the Dales and keen viewers might find bits of 'Darrowby' popping up in different places. Where you can be sure of finding something is at the Richmond Museum in Richmond, which has the original vet's surgery from the first television series on display (see p 28).

Hubberholme Church, Langstrothdale

❂ HUBBERHOLME

Down in a wooded valley, with a stream flowing by on its way to join the River Wharfe, the tiny 12th-century **Parish Church of St Michael and All Angels** is a true delight of the Dales. Originally a forest chapel, it's a small stone building, a church that seems to have shrunk in the rain. 'I was christened here and married here,' a visitor was heard to say, 'and, please God, I'll be buried here too.' The pews, choir stalls and chairs have been made by the famous wood-carver Robert Thompson, known as the Mouseman because of his characteristic signature of a carved mouse, which is often hard to find. Look for the South Altar too, which was used for many years as an ale bench in the village pub. The church was a favourite with Yorkshire author J B Priestley, and a plaque inside commemorates him. His ashes are scattered nearby, and the village pub, the George, just a few yards away over the bridge, was Priestley's favourite place to drink. He loved the whole Dales, but described Hubberholme as 'one of the smallest and pleasantest places in the world'. Few could argue.

If visiting Hubberholme – and you should – it's worth timing it so that you can eat at the **Buck Inn**, five minutes away in Buckden (0756-760227). It serves superior pub food, unpretentious and cheap, whether you choose the bar or the dining room. A large and imaginative vegetarian selection - spinach and mushroom lasagne, mushroom and nut fettuccine - , steak pie cooked in Theakston's Old Peculier, a wide range of fish dishes. Even a simple salad is full of surprises, with nuts and fresh exotic fruits hidden among the greenery. Meals served daily from noon-2pm all year, and 6.30-9pm (9.30pm Friday and Saturday only) in summer, 7-9pm on Sundays and in winter.

☆ REETH

Reeth is an attractive village, sprawling around an enormous green, and tucked away down a back street is the building containing the excellent **Swaledale Folk Museum**. (To find it, stand at the top of the green with the Burgoyne Hotel behind you, and walk round the edge of the green to your left, then turn left.)

Museums devoted to one Dale are the best, taking pride in their history and gathering together the odd collections that make poking around some museums such fun. In this one you'll find a poacher's kit, including a ferret box, while the toy shop includes 'PANKO, or Votes for Women', a card game for suffragists vs anti-suffragists. There's a good lead-mining exhibit, reminding you that lead has been mined in these Swaledale hills for 1,000 years, while the inevitable sheep-farming display mentions that in 1989 a farmer in Arkengarthdale sold a tup he had bred for £30,000. Many of the exhibits are accompanied by some first-rate pencil drawings, which evocatively capture crafts like butter-making, or the crushing of lead ore for smelting.

Swaledale Folk Museum, Reeth Green, Reeth
Opening times: daily 10.30am-6pm

The **King's Head** pub on the green looks small from the outside but is very spacious inside, with one large bar and dining area that has lots of nooks, crannies and window seats. Theakston's ales and a good varied bar menu: home-made steak-and-kidney pies, shepherd's pies, local trout, vegetable lasagne. Food served daily: noon-2pm and 6.30-10.30pm.

The back road from Reeth leads up Arkengarthdale, past the villages of Booze and Whaw, high on to rugged moors and the Tan Hill Inn, the highest inn in England. It's an escape route from civilisation when the weather is fine, but it can be a desolate drive in bad weather, so be cautious if you're not used to the local conditions. It leads eventually to Kirkby Stephen, but an easier route is the B6270 along Swaledale and Birkdale (and passing the turning for the village of Crackpot).

Part-way along the B6270, Muker is the home of **Swaledale Woollens** (0748-86251), a cottage industry set up almost 20 years ago to encourage local knitting and develop the use of Swaledale wool. There is a fine collection of hand-knitted Swaledale sweaters, with many unusual designs and colours, cardigans, scarves and hats. There are also Swaledale tweeds, and several types of yarn available. If you are looking for a good woollen item, then this is one of the best places in the Dales to find it. Open Monday-Saturday 10am-5pm, Sunday 1-5pm.

☆ SEMER WATER

To the south of Bainbridge a winding rural road leads up to the village of Countersett and then down to Semer Water, the third largest natural lake in Yorkshire. It is the only remaining lake of several that were formed in this area during the Ice Age by the Great Wensleydale Glacier. Glaciers were also responsible for the many granite boulders visible in the pasture-land on the surrounding hill slopes.

Semer Water

Listen carefully when you visit the lake, in case you hear the sound of the church bells from the town that was drowned at the bottom. An angel came to earth disguised as a beggar, and despite a violent storm the villagers of the town refused to provide food or shelter. Eventually a shepherd in an isolated cottage took the angel in, but the next morning the angel took revenge by burying the rest of the town in what became Semer Water. Some would still like to take revenge on the water skiers and others who disturb the peace of the lake at weekends with the roar of boat engines. On weekdays your peace should be assured, so get out of the car, wander round the lake, and watch for the wildfowl and the many other birds that live here.

✪ WEST BURTON

West Burton is said by many to be the most beautiful village in the Dales, if not in the country. It is hard to argue with this. The enormous village green seems to go on forever, bounded on either side by old stone cottages. Children play on the green, on its edges horses graze, and in the centre is the Market Cross which dates from 1820 and commemorates the weekly market that used to be held here. What a fine sight that must have been.

Despite the drawback of living in a tourist attraction, the villagers maintain a remarkable friendliness, and a diversion to West Burton is not to be missed. At the bottom of the green, close by the one-way road that enters the village, a path leads to an old packhorse bridge and a small waterfall, known variously as Mill Force or West Burton Force.

West Burton – The village green and packhorse bridge

WHERE TO STAY

Appersett

Rigg House West, *Appersett, near Hawes, N Yorks DL8 3LR*
Tel: 0969-667712
Open all year
A detached house in an elevated position with stunning views over Wensleydale, Rigg House West offers a real bargain for those prepared to forgo a few minor comforts. All three double rooms share the same bathroom and separate WC, but the bedrooms are pleasant, filled with old wooden dressers and sideboards. Interesting objects fill the house: books, paintings, prints, sculptures, wooden carvings. The Dobermann which bounds out to greet arriving guests may look fierce, but is in fact quite a softie. The owner, Brenda Cheese, knows the countryside and can advise on walks for all conditions – of weather and walkers. She will even drive guests eight miles to the far end of the Lady Anne Clifford Trail, allowing them to walk back in time for supper. Good home cooking: soup or kipper pâté; chicken with tarragon or roast pork with juniper; apple crumble, cheese and coffee.

Hubberholme

� ⚹ ⚘ ✕ **££**

Kirkgill Manor, *Hubberholme,
Skipton, N Yorks BD23 5JE*
Tel: 0756-760800
Open all year
Along a narrow hedge-lined country
lane, Kirkgill Manor backs on to the
River Wharfe and was built in 1893
for the Vicar of Hubberholme. The
bedrooms are so large and comfortable, all with en suite bathrooms, that
there seems to have been a mistake in
the pricing. All are tastefully decorated in plain pastel colours. Dinner is
more a dinner party, with guests
gathered round a magnificent 12-
seater oak table at 7.30pm, tucking
into good home cooking: cream of
mushroom soup or melon cocktail
with port, baked Kilnsey trout or
pork en croûte with sage and bacon,
followed by a choice of puddings
and cheeseboard.

Reeth

⌂ ✕ ⚹ ⚘ ▬ **£££**

Burgoyne Hotel, *On the Green, Reeth,
Richmond, N Yorks DL11 6SN*
Tel: 0748-84292
Open all year
This beautiful 18th-century grey
stone building looks imposingly
down on Reeth's large green. The
eight bedrooms are bright, spacious
and tastefully decorated, some with

three windows overlooking the
Green. There are two lounges (one
non-smoking), and two dining
rooms, both looking on to the Green,
one reserved for residents. Good
food is a Burgoyne speciality. The
four-course dinner may include
chilled melon with peaches and
blackberries, or home-made fresh
salmon mousse to start, while main
courses will be fresh meat or fish
(salmon and spinach en croûte
Hollandaise, or slices of pork fillet
with apple and cider).

West Burton

⌂ ⚹ ✕ **£**

West Burton House, *West Burton,
Leyburn, N Yorks DL8 4JY*
Tel: 0969-663582
Open May - mid-Sept
Though only a modest family house,
with two rooms which are let out
only in season, this has to be recommended for the best view in West
Burton. The bedrooms are simply
furnished but large and spotlessly
clean, with a lounge for residents.
One room looks out on the wide
village green, the other back up
Wensleydale, an equally attractive
prospect. The two rooms share a
bathroom that's every bit as clean
and spacious as they are, and the low
cost makes it one of the bargains of
the Dales.

WHERE TO EAT

Askrigg

⌂ ✕ ▬ **£££**

The King's Arms, *Market Place,
Askrigg, Leyburn*
Tel: 0969-50258
Open daily, dinner only
The rough and ready bar you find as
you enter couldn't be more of a con-
trast to the lovely Clubroom
Restaurant upstairs. This is quail's

eggs and truffle country, and the
menu is priced accordingly. The
wine list is superb, as is the food.
Quail's eggs were served in a red
and white wine sauce, while an
unusual main course option was
chicken in a strawberry sauce served
with peppered strawberries. This
didn't quite come off, but it's good to
see surprises mixed in with tradi-

tional dishes – some recipes date from Georgian times. Expect to see local game and fish dishes, and try the cheeses, with delicious date and walnut bread. Last orders 9pm (8.30pm Sunday).

The nine bedrooms retain a wonderfully historic feel to them with canopied beds, tastefully done out in pinks and greys. It's a place to pamper yourself, provided you don't expect a typical hotel – the reception is more of a cupboard under the stairs!

Askrigg
✗ 📨 ££

The Rowan Tree, *Market Place, Askrigg, Leyburn*
Tel: 0969-50536
Closed Sun eve, Mon, & Tues lunch

Local food-lovers rave about The Rowan Tree, an intimate stone-walled room, subtly lit by candles and lamps. The fixed-price menu changes daily and is small enough to fit on a blackboard which is moved from table to table. Small scale with a good chef means superb food. Expect a starter such as carrot, ginger and coriander soup, served with home-made soda bread. Main courses include chicken with apple, sage and calvados or hot Wensleydale cheese soufflé with a grape and walnut salad. The puddings taste as good as they sound: coffee liqueur gâteau served with strawberries, peaches and kiwi fruit. The wine list could do with an injection of variety, but the service is friendly and this is a lovely place to spend a leisurely evening. Last orders: lunch 2pm, dinner 10pm.

Hawes
🏠 ✗ 🍽 ££

Herriot's, *Main Street, Hawes*
Tel: 0969-667536
Open daily

Locals speak highly of this ordinary-looking hotel and restaurant in the centre of Hawes – and the locals are right. Down some steps, the dining room is tastefully done out in burgundy and cream, with old tin advertising posters decorating the walls and shelves full of dusty books and bottles. The food is good, but not for faint hearts. Starters include a Dales country pâté or country mushrooms cooked in a port and mustard sauce, followed by generous main courses such as roast duckling or medallions of pork in a brandy, cream and mustard sauce. There is also a good selection of fresh fish dishes and steaks. Puddings may include sticky toffee pudding, dark and white chocolate slab and strawberry Pavlova. Last orders: lunch 2.30pm; dinner 9.30pm.

Sedbusk
🏠 ✗ 🍽 ££

The Stonehouse Hotel, *Sedbusk, Hawes*
Tel: 0969-667571
H open all year; R open dinner only, Easter - mid-Nov daily, otherwise Fri and Sat

At this small, quiet, country hotel, built in 1908, the fixed-price menu offers a choice of three or four dishes for each course. Starters may include a home-made soup and a country pâté. The pork in orange sauce was a superb, enormous cut of meat, so it wasn't surprising to discover that the family who run the hotel are also butchers. There's home-made bread, and the wine list is very reasonable, including some vintage bottles and a wide selection costing under £10. Last orders 8pm.

The bedrooms are decorated in various styles, with a tendency towards the floral but nothing too overpowering. The service is informal and relaxing, without being casual.

THE CUMBRIAN DALES

It might seem strange to find part of Cumbria in a guide to the Yorkshire Dales, but the dales themselves obey no county boundaries. The village of Dent, which some people claim is the most beautiful in the Yorkshire Dales National Park, actually has a Cumbrian address and its post goes via Lancaster! In fact when the Park boundaries were first drawn up, it was intended that the whole of this area should fall within the National Park. A change of heart excluded the northern half, but now discussions are taking place which may lead to the original plans being carried out at last. At the heart of this region is Mallerstang, known as the Magic Valley, through which flows the River Eden. It is one of the most beautiful yet lesser-known parts of Britain, and is a good place to spend the weekend if you want to escape the crowds.

If it rains the whole day can be spent visiting potteries, galleries, the Dent Crafts Centre and even a small weaving factory near Sedbergh. A family day out could take in the Rare Breeds Farm near Dent and include a ride on the wonderfully scenic Settle to Carlisle railway across remote landscapes, over viaducts and through long tunnels beneath the high moorland. A trip on the train also allows you to get off at any of its many stops for a walk or to visit one of the towns along its 72-mile route.

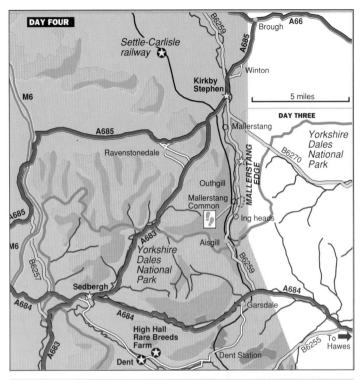

★ DENT

Dent is one of the most attractive villages in the Dales. Two typical old-fashioned English pubs face each other across a cobbled corner. Terraces of old stone cottages huddle together on narrow twisting cobbled streets. Most cottages face straight onto the street, so that sometimes you can see only a few yards ahead, then the street bends and the buildings suddenly act as a frame for green fields, a mile away on the other side of Dentdale, one of the smaller and more beautiful Dales. The sides of the valley aren't steep and sweeping, they're gentler and more wooded, giving greater variety to the scenery. Little wonder there's a small artistic community here.

Dent's charm does draw the crowds, of course, and it's one of the few places in the Dales that can get as busy as a Cotswold village, so try to get there early or late in the day. There is a large car park not far from the Stone Cross Café which contains a tourist information point. Park there or you will get caught up in the narrow winding streets. You could easily find yourself driving out of the other side of the village and unable to turn round for a mile or so on the narrow hedge-lined country lanes.

Dent has a large memorial stone to the naturalist Adam Sedgwick, who was born here in 1785. He attended Dent and Sedbergh schools, before going to Cambridge University where he eventually became Professor of Geology. For those interested in Sedgwick, or geology, there's an enjoyable walk called the 'Sedgwick Geological Trail', on the Sedbergh-Hawes road, for which we recommend you buy the appropriate leaflet in the Yorkshire Dales National Park Trail Series.

Dent's modern residents include musician Mike Harding, artist John Cooke and photographers John and Eliza Forder, whose beautiful books, *Hill Shepherd* and *Life in the Hills* are in every bookshop in the area. Both the Forders and John Cooke have small studios in Dent where their work is for sale. The Forders produce wonderful photographs of life in the Dales, in both colour and black and white, and if you can't afford an original print there are many small postcards as well as their books. John Cooke's work is varied but includes many distinctive oil landscapes, mainly of Dentdale and the Lake District, and if you buy one of his works you will have something in common with the Royal Family. If visiting, remember that these are studios rather than shops, so opening hours vary. The Forders' studio (tel: 05875-387) is behind the Sedgwick stone, and John Cooke is at the nearby Hill Studio (tel: 05875-354).

A short drive out of Dent at Helmside on the road towards Sedbergh is the **Dent Crafts Centre** (tel: 05875-400). This is a delightful place in a converted old barn, where local craftspeople and artists of all kinds exhibit and sell their work: leather, wood, candles, pottery, jewellery, photographs, paintings, baskets, screenprints... even pastry-work and plants. It's the kind of place where you find yourself wandering round picking up item after item, and realising you could easily empty your purse or wallet. Open 9.30am-6pm daily March - mid-January, weekends only mid-January - February.

HIGH HALL RARE BREEDS FARM

It's an adventure to find this farm near Dent, and another to visit it. Leave Dent on the lower of the two roads that lead eventually to Dent Station, and watch for the small sign on the left for High Hall Farm. The track up to the farm is very rough, so pray for your suspension. The two women who run the farm show people round according to demand, and the tour takes anything from an hour upwards. At quiet times you could be there all afternoon and end up feeding the animals. It's that kind of informal place.

The farm covers 65 acres, and you'll tramp over most of them meeting the 34 rare breeds of sheep, goats, horses, cattle and pigs that live there. The talk as you walk is always entertaining, especially when discussing the mating habits of some of the animals. It's all the more delightful for being a farm where the animals are loved and given acres of space, rather than being penned up just for visitors to look at. At the end you'll be offered a cup of tea or glass of juice, in the farm's makeshift 'café' (a back bedroom), setting you up for the bumpy ride back to civilisation.

High Hall Rare Breeds Farm, Dent, near Sedbergh. Tel: 05875-331
Opening times: daily except Tuesday 3-6pm
Admission: adult £2; child £1

High Hall Rare Breeds Farm, near Dent

☆ KIRKBY STEPHEN

Kirkby Stephen is still only slowly waking up to tourism, and the unusual **Parish Church of St Stephen** is its main attraction and something of a hidden delight... not to mention yet another candidate for 'The Cathedral of the Dales'. Not exceptional to look at from the outside, hemmed in as it is by the surrounding buildings, it nevertheless contains many treasures. A guide has been produced in the form of a large illustrated sheet, providing a nice souvenir of the church, with fine drawings of some of the more notable features. These include the 18th-century bread shelves, where bread was distributed to the poor of the parish through the terms of a local charity.

The church also houses the ancient Loki stone, a 10th-century cross shaft depicting the old Norse God, Loki. An interesting pulpit made of granite and Italian marble dates from 1871. Most moving of all, however, is a tribute to local men who died during World War II. This is a simple book, with a photograph of each

Pendragon Castle, Mallerstang

man, and an account of his short life given in a child's handwriting. It's a touching tribute, and those behind it should be proud of it.

In the churchyard, behind the cloisters which form the entrance to the church grounds, look for a large flat stone table. This is the Truppstone, on which tenants used to place their rent money until 1836. It's worth looking at the tombstones as well, which include many intriguing life stories, including tales of piracy.

(i) Kirkby Stephen's **Tourist Information Centre** is in Market Street (tel: 07683-71199).

> A few miles north of Kirkby Stephen is the **Langrigg Pottery** in Winton. This small pottery is usually open daily, 9am-5pm, but do telephone first to make sure, on 05873-71542. All work for sale is made on the premises, and includes an attractive range of mugs, plates, vases and jugs.

☆ MALLERSTANG

Known as the Magic Valley and running south from Kirkby Stephen, Mallerstang has magnificent scenery and is a lovely place for a drive or a walk.

The first main attraction south of Kirkby Stephen is **Pendragon Castle**, little more than a few strangely atmospheric ruins in a field at the side of the road. Built in the 12th century, the castle's first owner was Hugh de Morville, one of the knights who murdered Thomas Becket. It was burnt down by Scots raiding over the border, and rebuilt in 1660 by Lady Anne Clifford. It is said to have been named after Uther Pendragon, although sadly there is no evidence of buildings on this site before the 12th century. The field where the ruins stand is privately owned, but public access is permitted. It stands at the junction of the B6259 and the one minor road going off to the right, about three miles south of Kirkby Stephen.

A few miles further on is a cluster of houses forming the valley's only village, **Outhgill**, where you'll find **The Church of St Mary**. This is usually locked, but the key may be obtained from the house more or less opposite the entrance. Inside are some bread shelves, similar to the ones in Kirkby Stephen church, and

Outhgill Parish Council still administers a charity which provides loaves for anyone in the area over retirement age. Above the church door the following plaque is of interest: 'This chapple of Mallerstang after it had layne ruinous and decayed some 50 or 60 years, was newe repayred by the Lady Anne Clifford, Countesse Dowager of Pembroke, Dorsett & Montgomery, in the year 1663; who also endowed the same with lands which she purchased in Cawtley, near Sedbergh to the yearly value of eleaven pounds forever.' The church 'lay ruinous' more recently, too, and was 'newe repayred' by a group of local people and became a living church yet again. 'Boon Day' is another tradition still kept up – on the first convenient day after the end of hay-making, people gather in the churchyard to cut the grass and tend the graves.

About a mile south of Outhgill Church is the entrance to Ing Heads Farm, base for the **North of England Falconry and Conservation Centre**. This is in its early days yet, but has a flying area where birds of prey will be flown three times a day, weather permitting, with a classroom for educational visits (and wet weather) and light refreshments. The birds include lanner and lugger falcons, saker falcons, harris hawks and red-tailed hawks.

Open: daily, 10am-dusk. For times of flying displays each day, tel: 07683-72144
Admission: adult £2; child £1

Church of St Mary, Outhgill

View from Mallerstang Edge

MALLERSTANG EDGE WALK

A walk to the top of Mallerstang Edge is an exhilarating experience, and is on your doorstep if staying at The Thrang Hotel. If not, they won't mind if you park your car there as you'll be ready to use the tea-room when you get back down again. With the door to the tea-room behind you, walk along the main road for about 20 yards, and through the gate on the opposite side of the road. What may look to you like any other rutted farm track is in fact part of the Lady Anne Clifford Trail, an ancient Roman road which, if you can manage to follow it, leads up eventually to the Edge. From below, this looks like a ridge, but on top is a flat and grassy plateau where hundreds of skylarks nest. If you do find it hard to follow Lady Anne's trail, then simply pick your way as best you can up towards the Edge – and watch out for the peregrine falcons that nest on the cliffs. All the land here is open grazing land, so feel free to tramp up it, watching out for wheatears and sheep droppings.

At the top of the ridge are three stone markers indicating Hugh Seat, named after that first owner of Pendragon Castle, Hugh de Morville. If you look to the north the slightly higher ground is High Seat, which is your ultimate goal at just over 2,300ft. The walk up here can be boggy in wet weather, so either wear suitable footwear or be prepared to pick your way round the boggy parts. It is an exhilarating climb, reasonably easy if you're fit, and at the top you can gaze along the length of Mallerstang, watch for a train passing on the Settle-Carlisle line far below, and, even on a summer Saturday, you will probably be alone.

☆ SEDBERGH

Sedbergh is a market town, busy for its small size, with a typical Dales market every Wednesday whose original charter dates back to the 13th century. The town is at the conjunction of four valleys and four rivers so has some delightful open views over fields to distant hills, and there is good walking country around, notably the Howgill Fells. Check at the **National Park Centre** for walking leaflets. It has no major attractions by way of museums or craft shops, yet there are many minor delights that make it worth a few hours of anyone's time. St Andrew's Church retains some of its original Norman stonework, there are some grand 18th-century town houses along the cobbled Main Street and hidden alleyways leading to Tudor courtyards. Sedbergh School dates back to pre-Reformation times. William Wordsworth sent his son there, and Coleridge's son taught there, until he was dismissed for being drunk!

The Dalesman, an old stone country inn on Main Street (tel: 05396-21183) has a large stone-walled bar area and a separate Buttery restaurant serving generous helpings of good pub food. The large menu ranges from simple toasted sandwiches and jacket potatoes to local venison cooked in red wine with walnuts, celery and redcurrants, fresh salads and fish dishes. Children's menu. Last orders: lunch 2pm, dinner 9.30pm.

In the nearby village of **Brigflatts**, about a mile along the main road to Kirkby Lonsdale, there is a delightfully peaceful Friends' Meeting House in the form of an old cottage dating from 1675, with the surprising sight of a gallery running round three sides of its main room. Nearby is a churchyard where the Quaker George Fox once preached.

About a mile from Sedbergh, on the A684 towards Hawes, is a group of buildings called Farfield Mill, the home of **Pennine Tweeds**. Machinery dating from the 1930s is used to produce a range of blankets, ties, sweaters, hats, gloves and, of course, woollen tweed cloth itself. Owned and run by Bryan Hinton and his wife, whom you may or may not find weaving, its working hours are dictated by business rather than tourists, but visitors are more than welcome to wander in and watch the machinery at work or browse round the shop and buy from a wide range of cloth at wholesale prices. 'When dressmakers call in, they're amazed at the range of cloth they can buy,' Bryan Hinton says. 'Time and again we've had people from London saying they can buy stuff here that you simply cannot get in the shops in London or anywhere else.' Open daily, 10am-5pm, closed Sunday in winter (tel: 05396-20558).

THE SETTLE TO CARLISLE RAILWAY

Mallerstang, in particular, has always been an isolated dale, and the Settle-Carlisle railway has long been a vital part of the community, helping to keep up its few links with the outside world. The recent fight to ensure the railway's survival was particularly keen here.

The 72-mile-long Settle-Carlisle line was built entirely by manual labour between 1869 and 1876, at a cost of £3.5 million and many lost lives. It must have been like trying to build the Channel Tunnel with picks and shovels. The result was a magnificent feat of Victorian railway engineering, crossing rivers, valleys and moors in some of the grandest scenery in the country.

There are many viaducts along the line, the most famous and spectacular being the 24 arches of the Ribblehead Viaduct near Horton-in-Ribblesdale. The highest of its arches reaches 165ft, but there are viaducts almost as high at Dent Head and Arten Gill, both in Dentdale, and another in Settle which takes the tracks over part of the town.

The stretch of line north from Settle to Blea Moor, about 15 miles away, is known as the Long Drag, a slow uphill climb until the track plunges under Blea Moor through a $1\frac{1}{2}$-mile tunnel, the longest on the line. Truly one of the world's great train journeys.

Settle-Carlisle Railway

For the visitor, a ride will take you through some of England's finest scenery, giving everyone a break from the car and the driver a chance to look around at the view instead of watching for tractors and lunatic sheep. Some people plan their whole holidays around the line, leaving the car at home. From Settle there are easy links with Leeds, and from Carlisle with Glasgow.

The day-tripper based in Kirkby Stephen, say, could catch a train at about 8am and be walking round Skipton Castle an hour later, returning at any time during the afternoon. It gives a chance to travel through the Blea Moor tunnel and over the Ribblehead and Dent Head viaducts. If you plan to get off at Dent, however, note that the station is a few miles from the village (taxis can be booked on 05875-432/203). A popular story has a visitor asking a local why the station's so far from Dent. "Appen they wanted it near to t'track,' is the answer.

An up-to-date timetable is essential, and these are widely available at stations and tourist offices throughout the region. There are usually at least half a dozen trains a day in both directions, stopping at all stations. Rover tickets allow you to hop off and on at any station along the line. For information telephone: Leeds, 0532-448133; Bradford, 0274-733994; Skipton, 0756-792543; Carlisle, 0228-44711.

WHERE TO STAY

Dent

🛏 🕏 🍴 £

The Sun Inn *and* **The George and Dragon**, *Main Street, Dent, Sedbergh, Cumbria LA10 5QL*
Tel: Sun 05875-208, George 05875-256
Open all year
Dent's two pubs, owned by the same landlord, face each other across the cobbles of Dent's Main Street. The landlord has his own brewery, producing the deliciously nutty Dent Bitter, and a stronger brew called Ram's Bottom. 'You only drink that if you're staying here,' I was told, 'as you certainly couldn't drive home afterwards... even walking can be a bit tricky.' The rooms are basic and some are quite small, but they're clean and economical. Those at the George are of a slightly better standard. All rooms share bathrooms.

Kirkby Stephen

🏠 ✗ 🕏 🐴 🍴 ££

The King's Arms Hotel, *Kirkby Stephen, Cumbria CA17 4QN*
Tel: 0930-71378
Open all year; R dinner only
The King's Arms, a 17th-century former posting inn in the centre of Kirkby Stephen, provides what travellers have always needed: a comfortable bed, a good meal and a drink.

The downstairs bars serve food daily and are small and popular with locals. Upstairs is surprisingly spacious with 11 bedrooms of a decent size. Only three have en suite bathrooms. The bedroom furnishings are basic, reflected in the price, but compensating features include the walled garden and a dining room with antique furniture and tapestries. The restaurant offers a four-course menu that tends to stick to plain dishes but does them very well. Starters include a home-made soup, the main course might be roast leg of lamb with mint sauce or salmon pie in filo pastry, followed by home-made puddings, with a small, good value wine list. Last orders: lunch 1.45pm; dinner 9pm.

Kirkby Stephen
ᾇ ✕ ⫟ᴵᴵ ⇥ 🖂 £££

The Town Head House, *High Street, Kirkby Stephen, Cumbria CA17 4SH*
Tel: 07683-71044
Open all year
This is a superb detached part-Georgian, part-Victorian town house just away from the centre of Kirkby Stephen, with old-fashioned features but every modern comfort too. The large bedrooms still have their original plasterwork, some have four-poster beds, others half- or full-canopy beds. Dinner is served in the candlelit dining-room, with its open fire in winter. This is open to non-residents too. Everything that can be home-made is home-made, including the bread, pâtés, ice-creams. Dinner might start with a soup or sardines gratinées, followed by sirloin steak, or rack of lamb chops with ginger and nut sauce. An unusual feature is the built-in wall safe. It was so well built-in that it proved impossible to

remove, and now serves as a drinks cabinet – let's hope they never forget the combination.

Mallerstang
ᾇ ✕ ⫟ᴵ ⇥ 🖂 ££

The Thrang Country House Hotel, *Mallerstang, Kirkby Stephen, Cumbria CA17 4JX*
Tel: 07683-71889
Open all year
'Just like being at home,' one visitor said, 'but with servants.' The Thrang is a Victorian house sympathetically modernised by owners Wyn and John Hamilton. There are lovely original stained glass windows, gothic-style doors and an unusual turret which acts as a general utility room for the bedrooms, with fridge, hoover, ironing board and tea-making facilities. The rooms vary in size but all are pleasantly furnished with antiques. There is said to be a ghost, an old lady who once lived here and who appears on the stairs. A guest having 'the powers' told the owners all about her: apparently the lady's amazed that people can go to the toilet in their own bedroom. The dining room is open to non-residents for an evening meal at 7.30pm. The food is usually simple but tasty and substantial, such as pork in cider or baked trout.

Ravenstonedale
ᾇ ✕ ⫟ᴵ ⇥ ▭ £££

The Black Swan, *Ravenstonedale, Kirkby Stephen, Cumbria CA17 4NG*
Tel: 05873-204
Open all year; R dinner only
More a country hotel than an inn, the Black Swan stands surrounded by village houses, its garden backing on to a stream. Its 16 spacious bedrooms

include three custom-built for the disabled, with doors opening onto the parking space directly outside. The Black Swan has its own first-class restaurant, which is non-smoking, as is one of the lounges. There's also a games room, a smart cocktail bar and a homelier local bar.

The food is as good as it sounds: freshwater eel from the Black Swan's own tarn, oak-smoked and served with salad and spiced mayonnaise, or slices of pudding pears oven-baked with fresh cream and stilton. A sorbet or soup will follow, and the main course will be served with vegetables that, where possible, have been organically grown in the village. The wine list has many good value wines, and a pricier cellar selection. Last orders: 9.30pm.

Sedbergh
ⓖ 🏃12 🏮 ££
Marshall House, *Main Street, Sedbergh, Cumbria LA10 5BL*
Tel: 05396-21053
Open all year

If you enjoy old houses then Marshall House is quite a surprise. It would be easy to pass it by as just another house on Sedbergh's narrow Main Street, yet it is a listed building, originally built around 1730, and inside has many fine original features: oak panelling, a grand staircase, coved ceilings and, in places, even some 18th-century plumbing! Below the house is a 16th-century

vaulted cellar and outside a walled garden with a stream and wonderful open views. The three bedrooms are plainly decorated but large and comfortable. Rooms on the ground floor are suitable for the disabled. If you're a keen walker then the owners, Mr and Mrs Kerry, are happy to offer advice and lend their own maps.

Sedbergh
🏠 ✕ 🏃8 ▭ ££
Oakdene Country House Hotel, *Garsdale Road, Sedbergh, Cumbria LA10 5JN*
Tel: 05396-20280
Open Mar-Dec; R dinner only

This handsome house set in an acre of land looks like a Victorian vicarage, but was built in 1880 for the Dover family, who were then the leading mill owners in Sedbergh, a mile away. Many of the house's original features have been retained, including gas lights and fine marble fireplaces. There's a lounge and a licensed restaurant, with lovely views of the surrounding fells. The restaurant is open to non-residents and offers a simple, wholesome and very reasonably priced three-course meal. Starters include home-made soup, fruit juice, fresh salmon or pâté with toast, while main courses are along the lines of breaded haddock, roast beef and Yorkshire pudding, baked ham in a cheese sauce or a cold meat salad. Last orders: 9.30pm.

WHERE TO EAT

Dent
✕ ▭ £

The Hop Bine Restaurant, *Dent Crafts Centre, Helmside, Dent, Sedbergh Tel: 05875-400*
Open all year, Fri-Mon, dinner only
On four nights a week the Dent Craft Centre's café becomes the Hop Bine Restaurant. It is a delightfully informal place of stripped-pine tables and bright table-cloths, the walls filled with paintings and photographs. The fixed-price four-course meal, with coffee and mints, is good value. There's a slight leaning towards healthy eating and always a vegetarian main dish. A typical meal might include grapefruit in crème de menthe, Teviotdale beef pie and peach and pear crumble. Small inexpensive wine list. Booking is essential and there are regular musical events too. Last orders: 8.30pm.

Dent
✕ ▭ £

The Stone Close Café, *Main Street, Dent, Sedbergh Tel: 05875-231*
Open all year
Located in a 17th-century listed building, once two farm cottages, in the centre of Dent. The daytime menu tends towards the needs of Dentdale hikers with such delicious dishes as farmer's hot pot and beef and bacon loaf. Food is served all day, with last orders being around

5.15pm. In the evening there's one sitting at 7.30pm, when the menu will include more unusual dishes: fish pâté with oatcakes or mushroom tartlets. The wine list is limited but reasonable priced, with a few surprises such as elderflower and gooseberry. Virtually no choice on the dinner menu, but you can guarantee that whatever you're given will be special.

Kirkby Stephen
✕ ▭ £

The Old Forge Bistro, *39 North Road, Kirkby Stephen Tel: 07683-71832*
Open all year, closed Mon
Originally a 17th-century smithy, now an unpretentious bistro which opens at 5.30pm in the evening. The basic menu is fairly predictable but is livened up by daily specials such as cheesy courgette and pineapple flan, plaice stuffed with prawns and mushrooms and a chicken tikka masala. The standard 'Old Forge Salad' is delicious, a fruit-bean-nuts-greens concoction, and the filling puddings include the staple Dales sticky toffee pudding, and an old-fashioned treacle sponge with custard. A limited but low-priced wine list helps make for a cheap and cheerful night out, evidently very popular with locals. Last orders: 10pm.

THE THREE PEAKS
DISTRICT

The scenery of this south-west corner of the Yorkshire Dales is the most dramatic, containing as it does the three highest peaks in the region: Whernside, Pen-y-Ghent and Ingleborough. If you're feeling fit and the weather's fine, there can be few more exhilarating feelings than reaching the top of any of the three and enjoying the magnificent views. You needn't go to the extremes of the fell-runners, however, whose challenge is to get to the top of all three in the same day. The Three Peaks Race is usually held in April or May each year.

As well as scaling the peaks, you can also descend to the depths and visit Ingleborough Cave near Clapham and - the best cave network in the Dales - the White Scar Caves. Both are more breathtaking if there has been some rain, filling the underground rivers that flow through them, but torrential rain can close the caves completely. If the weather is really against you then you can head for Settle with its museum, good shops and eating places.

On a fine day you could work up an appetite on the Ingleton Waterfalls Walk, which is justifiably one of the most popular walks in the Dales, then take a lunch break at Ye Olde Naked Man café in Settle, and in the afternoon see the Yorkshire Dales Falconry Centre in nearby Giggleswick, with its thrilling flying displays.

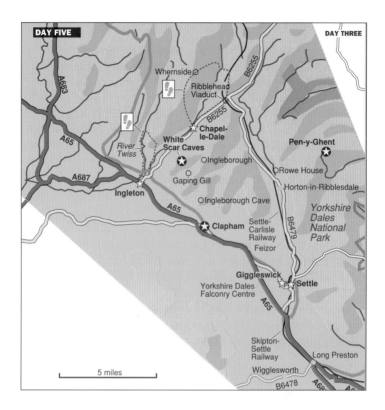

DAY FIVE

DAY THREE

Whernside

Ribblehead
Viaduct

B6255

A683

B6255

Chapel-
le-Dale

A65

River
Twiss

White
Scar Caves

Pen-y-Ghent

Ingleborough

A687

Gaping Gill

Rowe House

Ingleton

Horton-in-Ribblesdale

A65

Ingleborough Cave

Yorkshire
Dales
National
Park

Clapham

Settle-
Carlisle
Railway

B6479

Feizor

Giggleswick

Settle

Yorkshire Dales
Falconry Centre

A65

5 miles

Skipton-
Settle
Railway

Long Preston

Wigglesworth

B6478

☆ CHAPEL-LE-DALE

The beautiful 17th-century **Chapel of St Leonard** at Chapel-le-
Dale is a lovely little place less than 50ft long. It is well worth
visiting for its stained glass alone, most of which is original.
Note also the moving plaque to the men who lost their lives
building the Settle-Carlisle railway, whose Ribblehead Viaduct is
nearby. By the door is a gravestone to the memory of Tom and
Isobella Ellen Kilburn of the nearby Hill Inn. What tragedy lies
behind the fact that they died together, aged 60 and 55, on 11th
January, 1928? And what does the anchor draped round the
cross on their tombstone signify? A little research would uncov-
er the story, but the visitor might find it more haunting to leave
it unresolved. Also buried here is caver Christopher Long, who
discovered the White Scar Caves down the road.

⊛ CLAPHAM

Clapham is an attractive little village with 18th-century houses running alongside a tree-lined stream crossed by hump-backed bridges. A few waterfalls are still used to provide hydro-electric power. Clapham Church has a 12th-century tower, though is otherwise of unexceptional modern design, mainly Regency, and the village has a few small shops and cafés. There's also a **National Park Centre**, and a delightful woodland walk of a mile or so to the **Ingleborough Cave**.

The path to the cave is well marked from Clapham village, and a charge of a few pence is made in order to enter the Ingleborough Estate. The walk to the cave is the first part of the **Reginald Farrer Nature Trail**, and a leaflet showing the full route is available from the National Park Centre. Ingleborough Hall, which is hidden away well off the trail, was bought by Oliver Farrer, a wealthy lawyer, in the 1760s. In 1880 Reginald Farrer was born there, and he went on to become one of the most famous botanists of the early 20th century, known as 'the Father of English Rock Gardening'. He travelled to the Alps, Ceylon, Japan, Tibet and Burma, among other places, and brought back a wide variety of plants and trees which he then planted on the estate. These are not labelled, so you need to know what you're looking for, or at, but you can still find many Alpine rock plants, Japanese maples, exotic azaleas and ten or so species of rhododendron out of the 24 species that were originally brought back.

Try to reach Ingleborough Cave for the first tour of the day at 10.30am, which is usually the quietest. Nothing of great significance has been found in the cave network, although it is still being expanded and at Fox Holes cave, 400 yards away, evidence of a Neolithic settlement has been discovered. You enter the cave as if through the back door, under a ledge of rock. Inside the light is kept fairly dim, with main features being spot-lit. One of these is the so-called Sword of Damocles, which is said to be the longest stalactite in the country at 5ft (and growing, of course.) It is a little unnerving to walk underneath this massive pointed stone, supported as it is by just four smaller stalactites.

There are also unusual rock shapes to spot: the jockey's cap, witch's fingers and the coffee pot among them. The Pool of

Reflections is a quite beautiful feature, with a distant rock formation resembling a mythical city, rising out of and mirrored in the still dark water. At one point the guide will switch out all the lights, to show you what total blackness is like – an unnerving feeling, and you're glad when the lights go back on again. The guides are helpful and informative, well worth a tip at the end of the 50-minute tour.

Ingleborough Cave, Ingleborough Estate, Clapham. Tel: 04685-242
Opening times: daily Mar 1-Oct 31, otherwise weekends only. Tours run hourly from
10.30am to 5.30pm
Admission: adult £2.20; child £1.20

A longer walk can be made by going beyond the cave to take in Gaping Gill pothole and the peak of Ingleborough. The walk takes about six hours, so with an hour at the cave it's an all-day excursion for serious walkers and you'll need to provide yourself with food, boots, waterproofs and a compass. The Yorkshire Dales National Park leaflet 'Gaping Gill and Ingleborough' gives details of history, geology, viewpoints, safety instructions and a full route map based on the Ordnance Survey map.

> **Gaping Gill** is the most famous pothole in the Dales. Fell Beck, which runs so leisurely through Clapham, here plunges into the gaping dark mouth of the pothole and falls over 350ft down into the main chamber. This chamber is said to be big enough to accommodate the whole of York Minster, but to be lucky enough to view the awesome sight you must either be an experienced caver or arrange to be at Gaping Gill on a Bank Holiday weekend. That's when local caving clubs set up a winch and wind visitors down for a view of this spectacular, breath-taking scene.

Ingleborough is second highest of the three peaks, at 2,373ft, and although the walk from Clapham is the longest of the various paths to its summit, it is also the most attractive, at first through mixed woodland of yew, beech, oak and ash, then past the Ingleborough Cave and on through pot-holed moorland beyond Gaping Gill to the summit which you can see beckoning for much of the route. The shortest walk up is from Hill Inn, near Chapel-le-Dale.

Ingleborough and Settle-Carlisle Railway

☆ GIGGLESWICK

If you drive through Giggleswick on the main road, there doesn't look to be very much to it, but it's worth stopping and wandering round the back streets as there are some lovely old 17th-century cottages in the village proper. St Alkelda's parish church goes back even further, to the 15th century, the unusual name being that of a Saxon princess who was martyred. The village is also known for its public school, founded in the 16th century.

Founded rather more recently, in 1991, was the **Yorkshire Dales Falconry Centre**. It's entered from the A65 which by-passes Giggleswick, and has been known to cause consternation amongst passing motorists who suddenly see a Griffon Vulture with a 7ft wing-span circling above them. The vulture is Ringo, the only bird of its size flying in this country. Likewise, no other centre at the moment flies the beautiful Bataleur Eagle. Both are star turns at the centre's daily flying displays. These last for 30-45 minutes, varying according to the size of the crowd, the birds being flown and the weather. The display compares very well with those at other falconry centres. It's hard to imagine anyone not being thrilled at the sight of a peregrine falcon swooping in, as fast as any car, and skimming the heads of the crowd with its perfectly controlled flying.

Yorkshire Dales Falconry Centre, Giggleswick –
Ringo, the Griffon Vulture, and the Bataleur Eagle

There is a large gift shop and a café, with a lecture room upstairs where talks can be given and videos shown if wet. Outside there are a dozen or so birds on display – owls, buzzards, red-tailed hawks, falcons – and although it's always sad to see birds of prey confined to cages, the conservation value of falconry centres is inestimable.

The Yorkshire Dales Falconry and Conservation Centre, Crows Nest, on A65, near Giggleswick. Tel: 07292-5164
Opening times: daily except Christmas Day, 10am-dusk. Flying displays: noon, 1.30pm, 3pm and 4.30pm. Feeding time: 4-4.30pm
Admission: adult £3.50; child £2.50

☆ INGLETON

Ingleton is a small but pretty town, standing above a little wooded valley where two rivers meet. There are some steep streets down to the river, and it has what must be the smallest market in the Dales – no more than half a dozen stalls. It is a good base for walkers: the summit of Ingleborough is a comfortable 3½ mile walk from here. The Ingleton **Tourist Information Centre** is at the Community Centre in the Car Park on Main Street (tel: 05242-41049).

For real northern fish and chips try the **Inglenook Licensed Fish Restaurant** in The Back Square. The fish - cod, haddock and rock - is fresh, well-cooked and portions are generous. Open daily in summer, lunchtimes and evenings, but phone ahead in winter on 05242-41195.

In the Ingleton **Parish Church of St Mary's** the so-called Vinegar Bible is on permanent display in a small case. This has one of those great religious misprints: The Parable of the Vineyards has become The Parable of the Vinegar. The Norman font is now all that remains of the original church on this site. Ironically this was preserved because it was destroyed, having been rolled down the nearby hill and into the river at a time when the Doctrine of Baptism had been repudiated. It lay under the water until its restoration in 1830, its fine carvings still intact.

👣 INGLETON WATERFALLS WALK

This walk can be safely recommended as being within most people's capabilities, and it is sure to impress. Signs in the town direct you down through the winding streets to the riverside car park near the viaduct, where the waterfall trail begins. The car park is generally open from about 9.30am every day, and there's a charge for cars and walkers. Locals are no doubt well aware that you can do the walk the 'wrong' way round for free, though technically you should have a ticket: someone has to pay for the upkeep of the paths and fences. The full route is about five miles, and takes from 2½ to four hours on a well-marked footpath. Wear sturdy shoes as the path can be wet and slippery in places with the spray from the falls. You don't need a map, apart from for a short stretch half-way round, which isn't well signposted, and which is explained below.

Begin by walking alongside the River Twiss, through damp woodland, watching for wrens, dippers and wagtails. It's a while before you reach the first falls, but once you do they come thick and fast. At the Pecca Twin Falls the river tumbles into a wide

Ingleton Waterfalls Walk

pool and splits its way round a huge boulder that creates the twin falls. Beyond that is the narrow Hollybush Spout, with many other minor falls in between. The last fall on this part of the walk is Thornton Force, which falls 40ft over limestone rocks into a pool surrounded by a natural amphitheatre. Here you can pause and picnic, or braver souls can make their way to stand behind the fall itself.

Above Thornton Force is a farm track, on which you turn right, walking past a couple of farms – and perhaps calling in at Twistleton Hall for a real farmhouse tea or snack. Walk through the farmyards, alongside a wall, then veer left down a steep slope through a field towards a gate in the wall at the bottom. Cross over the road and the signposts for the Waterfalls Walk guide you again from then on.

This second part of the walk takes you down a ravine formed by the other river which runs through Ingleton, the River Doe. Here the rocky gorges are much steeper, and in one place the sides almost meet. A bridge has been built across the ravine for viewing purposes. It's perfectly safe though still giddy-making as you look down at the water thundering past, 30 feet beneath you. The path now makes its way down Baxenghyll Gorge back into Ingleton – a thoroughly exhilarating morning or afternoon's walk.

✪ PEN-Y-GHENT

The looming Pen-y-Ghent forms a dramatic backdrop to the tiny but sprawling village of Horton-in-Ribblesdale. The village is often busy for its size, being situated on both the Pennine Way and the Ribble Way, and it has a small **Tourist Office** in the Pen-y-Ghent Café (tel: 07296-333).

The smallest of the three peaks, though by less than 150ft, the brooding shape of Pen-y-Ghent evokes the Dales far more than Whernside or Ingleborough. Its very un-Yorkshire name means 'hill of the border', dating from the days when this was the border of one of the ancient Welsh kingdoms. It now provides one of the north's most popular walks, and in addition the route up from Horton is on the Pennine Way, so don't expect solitude. You must also keep to the marked routes because, as in many places in the Dales, the tramping of too many feet is eroding the landscape.

The top of Pen-y-Ghent is easily reached from Horton in a circular walk of about six miles. There is a tarmac path to the north of Horton Church. After you cross a stile, walk alongside a wall for some distance, then cross a ladder-stile, this well-marked track meets up with the Pennine Way. As long as you remember to turn left towards the summit, you can't go far wrong! Once past the summit, follow the Pennine Way signs which direct you back by a different route into Horton.

 ## SETTLE

Settle is an historic market town, and for once that remark is not a cliché. Its Tuesday market was first held in 1249 and is still going strong. Here you'll find dozens of stalls selling meat, fish, cheeses, plants, records, shoes, jeans and gardening tools, amongst many other things, in a lively bustle with occasional buskers too.

In addition, Settle has several good eating places, antique shops, picture galleries, many buildings dating back to the late 17th century, arcaded buildings by the market square known as 'The Shambles' (formerly butchers' shops and a slaughterhouse) and a small museum.

(i) The **Tourist Information Centre** is in the Town Hall on Cheapside (tel: 07292-5192), the Town Hall itself being worth a look. It was built in 1833 and its unusual design has been described as Jacobean Gothic.

> The **Dales Picture Shop** is worth seeking out, at 6 Church Street, about 20 yards downhill from the market square. Many places sell local watercolours but this gallery has more unusual and attractive items, including photographs of life in the Dales, oil paintings, and some arts and crafts imported from France. Open 10am-5pm Monday-Saturday, but closed Wednesdays in winter; tel: 07292-3123.

 The **Museum of North Craven Life** may be tiny but it has enough of interest to make it worth a visit. One pleasing feature is a commentary you can hear as you wander round, based on interviews with old people about their lives as farmers. This is part of a local oral history project, and the tapes vary but they always try to have one playing.

There's an interesting exhibition on the solar eclipse of June 29th, 1927, the first visible in Britain for 200 years. Neighbouring Giggleswick was chosen by the Astronomer Royal for the official observatory, and the town had to cope with an invasion of 6,000 cars. Another display is on medicine in Settle – appropriately enough, given the 1991 BBC documentary series, *The Doctor*, which featured a Settle GP. There's an Edwardian bedroom, a feature on the Settle-Carlisle Railway and a copy of the Market Charter of 1708, which renewed the original charter of 1249. This means that soon Settle will be celebrating the fact that a market has been held there every single week for the last 750 years.

The Museum of North Craven Life, 6-8 Chapel Street. Tel: 0729-822854
Opening times: Easter-June, weekends and Bank Hols; Jul-Sept, Tues-Sun and Bank Hols. 2-5pm
Admission: adult 50p; child 25p

For a good Yorkshire lunch, try **Ye Olde Naked Man**, a bustling café on Market Place. It was once an inn, and the unusual name is believed to have been a skit on over-elaborate fashions. Those who didn't dress up to the nines came here. Soups, pies, pasties, jacket potatoes, sandwiches and salads are available all day, while at lunchtime extra dishes are added, such as Cumberland sausage with apple sauce, home-made steak pie, cauliflower cheese bake with leeks and sweetcorn. Leave time to visit the café's bakehouse next door for fresh bread or home-made cakes. In the interests of equality we should point out that there is also an Olde Naked Woman, about two miles away in Langcliffe, run on similar lines. Open daily except Wednesday, 9am-5pm, lunch menu available from noon-2.15pm.

Settle Market Place

Near the top of Whernside, 2,415ft

CLIMBING WHERNSIDE

If you have time to climb only one of the three peaks, then it may as well be the biggest, Whernside, which is 2,415ft. From the top there are wonderful panoramic views. In one direction the view is across Ribblesdale to Ingleborough, 5 miles away, with the Ribblehead Viaduct looking like part of a toy train set in between. On the other side of the wall that runs along the top of the ridge are equally extensive open views up Deepdale towards Dent.

This full walk takes about four hours and allows you to pass the Ribblehead Viaduct of the Settle-Carlisle Railway, so that you can see how big it really is. Park near the Hill Inn, to the north of Chapel-le-Dale (making a detour to visit the church of St Leonard, if you have time). Almost opposite the Hill Inn is a lane which you follow for a few hundred yards until a smaller lane forks off to the left. Head to the left for about half a mile until the lane starts to peter out and you walk past a building on your right-hand side. You then cross another minor path, go over a ladder stile, and cross two large fields using two more ladder stiles, heading all the time up towards Whernside. You will eventually reach some artificial wooden steps placed in the hillside to prevent erosion – though they're so awkward to climb that many people walk round them, so adding to the problems. At the top of the steps you turn right along the ridge which leads you to the top of Whernside and a stunning view of Littledale below you, with Blea Moor beyond the railway.

If the walk up has tired you, then head back down by the same route to the car, because as yet this is only about one-third of the way. Most of the rest is downhill, though, and then along the flat. If carrying on, continue along the ridge keeping to the right of the stone wall. When you reach a stile, turn right to head downhill. The path here is not well marked and it's basically a case of picking your way down. Be warned that it can be boggy, so wellingtons or at least good boots are useful. If you head straight down you should pick up a path by a stream, Coal Gill, which will take you past a couple of delightful small waterfalls and back again on to a recognisable track, which turns right and goes over the railway. This path then runs by the side of the railway for about a mile, until it reaches the Ribblehead Viaduct. You then make your way to the road, turn right, and walk back about 1½ miles to the Hill Inn.

❂   WHITE SCAR CAVES

This is easily the best cave system in the Dales, and a must on any itinerary. The guided tour lasts about an hour and starting times vary but you shouldn't have too long to wait in summer. There's a gift shop with a selection of books, including *Yorkshire's Hollow Mountains* by W.R.Mitchell, recommended if you want to find out more about the history of the caves, and the first people to explore them. You could also pass the time with a cup of tea and a bacon butty in the café. As regards the weather, this is a case of swings and roundabouts. If it is very wet then the caves are more spectacular, with thundering underground rivers and a real feeling of excitement, as if entering a Jules Verne adventure. The underground waterfall that you hear long before you see it is alone worth the price of admission. However, if it's *too* wet then the further caves may be closed, as the rivers rise and flood the walkways. The admission price is reduced to compensate for this. In dry weather you see the whole network, but some of the underground rivers may dry up completely. As you enter there is a model of caver Christopher Long, crawling down the narrow shaft that originally led into the cave, which he discovered in 1923. You're asked to imagine what made him do it... crawling half-naked on hands and knees through a black wet tunnel for hours, lit only by a candle on his hat. Then you're told what did make him do it – but you ought to visit the caves to find out.

White Scar Caves, Ingleton. Tel: 05242-41244
Opening times: daily except Christmas Day, from 10am; last tour 5.30pm
Admission: adult £3.99; child £2

WHERE TO STAY

Feizor

Scar Close Farm, *Feizor, Austwick, via Lancaster LA2 8DF*
Tel: 0729-823496
Open all year
Scar Close is a working farm, a few miles from Settle, and the accommodation is in a former Dales barn which was completely re-built in 1985. Because it was purpose-built, the three spacious rooms all have en suite bathrooms and modern furnishings and compare favourably with many modern hotel rooms at three times the price. The hamlet of Feizor is attractive, surrounded by woods, farmers' fields and limestone cliffs - the kind of place for those who like walks on the doorstep.

Horton-in-Ribblesdale

The Rowe House, *Horton-in-Ribblesdale, near Settle, N Yorks BD24 0HT*
Tel: 0729-860212
Open all year
In a lovely setting at the foot of Pen-y-Ghent, Rowe House is a late 18th-century shooting lodge. Some of the six bedrooms are slightly small, though not uncomfortably so, and they have all the facilities you might want in a guest house. A great attraction is the home-produced food. Breakfast includes free-range eggs, and honey from their own hives. Dinner always includes a vegetarian course, home-grown vegetables where possible, and dishes such as oven-baked Wharfedale trout with herbs, served with a lemon and wine sauce, or poached chicken with mushroom sauce.

Ingleton

Ingleborough View, *Main Street, Ingleton, N Yorks LA6 3HH*
Tel: 05242-41523
Open all year
Though the house is in Main Street the traffic has been diverted, so it's quiet with a view down to the river at the back and a five-minute stroll to the start of the Ingleton Waterfalls Walk. The house is in one of those indistinct rows of detached and semi-detached houses, and inside it is a typical friendly British B&B. The three bedrooms are a good size, and while the floral decor may not be to everyone's taste they are spotlessly clean. They share two spacious bathrooms.

Settle

Cromwell House, *Moor Lane, Long Preston, Skipton, N Yorks BD23 4QH*
Tel: 0729-840246
Open all year
Once the home of writer Jilly Cooper,

this is a small but very comfortable non-smoking guesthouse, recommended by a rival as the best in the district! In a quiet lane on the edge of the village, the house was built in 1685 and modernised to keep many original features, such as the oak beams and huge fire surrounds. The three bedrooms are all large, plainly decorated, with private bathrooms. Dorothy Hutton is a professional caterer, so the food is above average, although there's no choice on the evening menu unless by arrangement. A typical dinner would be home-made soup, goujon of chicken in coriander with cashew nuts, pudding, cheeseboard, coffee and mints.

Settle
🏠 ✕ 🏃 🐕 ▭ ££££

The Falcon Manor, *Skipton Road, Settle, N Yorks BD24 9BD*
Tel: 0729-823814
Open all year; Ingfield Restaurant dinner only, and Sun lunch

In an imposing position as you drive into Settle from Skipton, the Falcon Manor was built in 1841 and has lovely rear gardens. The 21 bedrooms, a mixture of old and new, are all spacious and mostly decorated in relaxing pastel shades. They vary from standard to de-luxe, including the handsome Elgar Suite with four-poster bed and whirlpool bath. The staff are friendly without being over-familiar, and the restaurant, bar and lounges are all relaxing. Traditional, impeccable but informal. The restaurant is also traditional, serving the likes of roast lamb, sirloin steak, salmon and Dover sole. There's the occasional dash of flair, such as venison slices cooked with cranberries and whisky, and five vegetarian dishes. While you won't be surprised, you won't be disappointed either. Last orders: lunch 2pm; dinner 9.30pm.

WHERE TO EAT

Clapham
🏠 ✕ ▭ ££

The New Inn Hotel, *Clapham,*
Tel: 05242-51203
Open all year; R dinner only
This large 18th-century coaching inn is the traditional mix of small hotel, restaurant and pub, with a superior bar menu available at lunchtime and evenings. The restaurant dining room looks across Fell Beck to the old Clapham cottages beyond. There is a very reasonable fixed price four-course menu: starters such as herrings in madeira or melon with port; main courses such as salmon with cucumber sauce, cheese and leek pie or unusual but delicious grilled lamb chops on a bed of tropical fruit. Puddings are conventional, and the wine list pleasingly wide at average restaurant prices. The food is much better than the accommodation, which is basic and cheap. Last orders: lunch 1.45pm; dinner 9pm.

Settle
✕ ▭ ££

The Blue Goose, *Market Square, Settle*
Tel: 0729-822901
Open every day
Located behind the Shambles on the Market Square, this restaurant should establish a good reputation if it sorts out a few teething problems. The vegetarian dish was superb, but didn't need another plateful of identical vegetables. The wine list was small but cheap enough and this may improve. That apart, the food from the German chef-owner was delicious. There are three different fixed-price menus, and an à la carte menu. Excellent appetisers included a mouthwatering chicken and walnut soup. Main courses cover fish and grills with, naturally, roast goose, served with an apricot compote and brandy sauce. The one large dining area is tastefully done out in blue and white with dried flower arrangements breaking up the cool lines. Last orders: lunch 2.30pm; dinner 9.30pm.

Settle
🏠 ▭ ££

The Royal Oak, *Market Place, Settle*
Tel: 0729-822561/823102
Open all year
A well-established pub and restaurant which sets local standards, this is a traditional stone inn whose panelled lounge has a few dozen copper-topped tables and acres of space. A comfortable place in which to eat your Dales stew and dumplings, fish, or gloriously fattening puddings like the Yorkshire fat rascal (puff pastry filled with currants and demerara sugar, served with whipped cream.) The bar area also serves afternoon tea, 3.30-5.30pm. In the evenings dinner is also served in a more formal dining room with a huge oak fireplace and portraits lining the walls. The cooking could be called superior but safe: pepper steak, chicken en croûte, poached fillet of Scottish salmon with shrimp sauce. Nothing too adventurous, but good meat dishes, served with style. Last orders: lunch 2pm; dinner 10pm.

Wigglesworth
🏠 ▭ ££

The Plough Inn, *Wigglesworth, Skipton*
Tel: 07294-243
Open all year; R dinner only, closed Mon
This large and light conservatory behind the Plough, an 18th-century coaching inn in a quiet village, has views for miles in every direction. The pastel decor and cane chairs add to the relaxing atmosphere. The fixed-price menu offers good value. Starters range from home-made soup to a terrine of venison and pistachio nuts served with a confit of onion and grenadine. Main courses may include braised steak casseroled in Murphy's Irish Stout or rabbit pie. Puddings are home-made and vary with the season. Last orders 10.30pm. There are 12 large bedrooms with en suite bathrooms, beautifully decorated in light pastel shades. Those at the back have wonderful views of Pen-y-Ghent and Ingleborough. Downstairs real log fires burn in the panelled bars, and packed lunches are available for those walkers fired by the sight of the peaks.

SKIPTON AND SURROUNDS

This compact area in the south of the Dales has a range of rich possibilities for the visitor. It includes the lively market town of Skipton, the beautiful Bolton Abbey Estate and one of Britain's most visited villages, Malham, with gorges, waterfalls, rivers and a lake all within walking distance. Here the scenery is a little less lush than it is further north, but it's no less beautiful. Even a drive along this stretch of the busy A65, which runs from Leeds to the Lakes, is a visual treat, reminiscent in parts of Austria.

Rain or shine, outdoor types should make for the Malham area, where you can easily escape the crowds and head in to some of the most rugged scenery in the whole of the Dales. Nearby are the natural attractions of Malham Cove, Malham Tarn, Gordale Scar and Janet's Foss, all set in a magnificent landscape of grey limestone rock formations. For families, and those whose limit is a stroll, Bolton Abbey, owned by the Duke and Duchess of Devonshire, is the place to head for. Children will also enjoy a short ride on the Embsay Steam Railway and a visit to Kilnsey Park to feed the fish and ducks. Skipton is the main rainy-day option, with its large market, good shopping, castle, church and museum. You won't exhaust these possibilities in one day, though you may exhaust yourself trying.

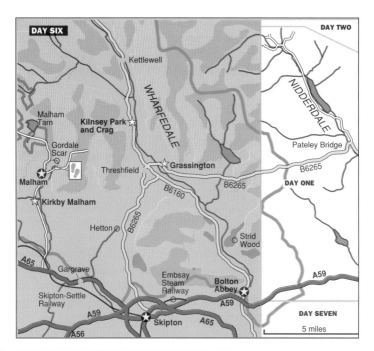

⊛ BOLTON ABBEY

In about the year 1155 a group of Augustinian monks walked, in their distinctive black robes, across the hills and moors from Embsay, four miles away, to found Bolton Abbey. Over 800 years later, much of the priory that they started to build still stands, overlooking the River Wharfe. The village of Bolton Abbey grew up around the priory, the land eventually passing to the Dukes of Devonshire, and the present Duke and Duchess still own the estate, much of which is open to the public.

The grounds also contain four car parks to cope with the many visitors, restaurants, a pub, a hotel, riverside walks and nature trails and several shops, including one which sells fencing materials from the estate sawmill. You'll be given a much-needed map when you park in one of the official car parks. It is best to use these parking facilities as there are precious few places otherwise. The roads around the village are mostly little country lanes, much used by tractors and other farm machinery, so badly-parked cars on the verges are not likely to be appreciated. The narrow stone arch which crosses one of the roads was built by the monks in order to bring water from a moorland stream to operate their flour mill.

A visit to the **Priory Church of St Mary and St Cuthbert** and the attached priory ruins is a must. It describes itself justifiably as one of the jewels of the north of England, and it's hard to know which is the more impressive, the church that's still in use or the crumbling walls that stand alongside looking over the river to the woods beyond. You can still make out the cloisters, chapter house and prior's lodging, though a guidebook bought in the church will help. The church was originally built in 1220, and its venerable age helped it escape total destruction during the Dissolution of the Monasteries, though it eventually fell into disrepair in the 1970s as the congregation dwindled to single figures. However, it now holds services again after a marvellous restoration job in the 1980s. It is well-manned with guides, so ask one of them to show you round.

You can't fail to be impressed by the six magnificent south windows, which were designed by the architect Augustus Pugin in 1853 and tell the complete gospel in 36 scenes, from the

Bolton Abbey: Bolton Priory and the River Strid

Annunciation to Pentecost. If you visit when the sun is shining, the pale stone of this graceful church is awash with rippling colours. The 1880 painting on the east wall is as fresh as if it were done today, with five Madonna lilies alternating with symbolic plants such as olive, vine and palm.

One of the other main attractions on the estate is the river, which is the Wharfe but is known for this stretch as the Strid. That's because it narrows into ravines that you can almost stride across, over the thundering white waters beneath - not recommended however, as many have tried and failed to make the jump, falling to their deaths on the boulders below.

The **Strid Wood Nature Trails** are riverside and woodland walks. They're beautiful, certainly, but also extremely popular so don't expect total solitude. The quietest seems to be the blue trail - you're given a map showing the walks of varying lengths when you arrive - which heads up and away from the River Strid, and hence attracts fewer visitors. Most seem to prefer to head straight for the water, to picnic on the rocks and admire the fast-flowing river with its miniature rapids and falls.

Despite the visitors, this area still flourishes as a nature reserve and is recognised as a Site of Special Scientific Interest. There are 62 known species of birds, from herons to wrens, 80 species of lichen, 97 of fungi, 98 of moss... and about two million species of visitor. The woods are predominantly beech and sycamore, and a noticeboard contains a sheet prepared monthly by the Wharfedale Naturalists' Society letting you know what birds, flowers, butterflies and even bees you might expect to see. Would you know a buff-tailed bumble bee if you saw one?

There's a cafeteria at the Cavendish Pavilion car park, serving a decent range of hot snacks and more substantial meals, mostly fish dishes. The Duke's Arms pub menu features game pie, pork hotpot and a salad bar but gets very crowded, so arrive before 12.30pm if you want a seat for lunch. Next door is the very upmarket Devonshire Arms Hotel Restaurant (see Where to Stay), which will cost you rather more than a simple pub lunch.

Bolton Abbey, on B6160, 12 miles from Skipton. Tel: 0756-710533
Opening times: grounds always open, but car parks and other facilities open daily,
including Christmas, dawn-10pm
Admission: £2 a car

☆ GRASSINGTON

Grassington is an attractive and bustling place, full of cobbles and 18th-century cottages, and of visitors. Its main appeal lies in the surrounding country, with good walking on Grassington Moor, and an interesting history of lead-mining. There's not too much in the town itself: accommodation and eating places, a **National Park Centre** and the tiny **Upper Wharfedale Museum** in the main square. The museum occupies half a dozen rooms in two old cottages, and while there are no outstanding exhibits to make it worth travelling to see, it will pass an idle half-hour on a rainy day. It does have quite a wide collection of local flints and minerals, the inevitable Dales farming exhibits, and a selection of veterinary tools which make you glad you're not a sheep. You couldn't fault the enthusiasm of the attendant, however, who doubles up as guide and puts the kettle on for tea or coffee should anyone ask.

Upper Wharfedale Museum, The Square, Grassington. Tel: 0756-752800
Opening times: 2-5pm, Apr-Oct daily, Nov-Mar Sat and Sun only
Admission: adult 40p; child 30p

☆ KILNSEY PARK AND CRAG

Kilnsey Crag is a huge limestone crag that looms out of the sur-rounding cliff-face towards the main B6160 road, causing not a few traffic hold-ups as drivers stop to stare. It's the finishing post for the August Bank Holiday Fell Race, rock-climbers use it for practice and soap opera fans should recognise it as featuring from time to time in the background of outdoor scenes on *Emmerdale*.

Children are likely to prefer Kilnsey Park, a small farm cum fish-ery a few hundred yards down the road. Parking is free and the small entry fee includes an equally small bag of feed for the rain-bow trout (that's if the dozens of ducks don't get to it first). As well as the trout and the numerous ducks – and let's admit it, everyone likes feeding ducks – there are Vietnamese and Peruvian pot-bellied pigs, a token length of dry-stone wall (though it's interesting to see some of the features explained, such as cripple holes), an adventure playground, a fly-fishing pond, a mini aquarium and a visitors' centre, with a choice of natural history videos to watch and a display showing farming life in the Dales. The place is *quite* interesting, and you may as well pop in as you're sure to be driving past Kilnsey Crag at some point, but you can't help feeling that with a little more effort it would actually be worth going out of your way to see.

Kilnsey Park, near Skipton. Tel: 0756-752150
Opening times: daily, 9am-5.30pm (or until dusk in winter)
Admission: adult £1.25; child 90p

Kilnsey Crag

☆ KIRKBY MALHAM

If the crowds at nearby Malham get too much for you, then peace and quiet is easily found a few miles away in the smaller village of Kirkby Malham. There's a lovely, uphill, walk out of the village on the Hanlith road, which begins opposite the pub and is marked 'No Through Road'. Keep walking till you get up high, and can enjoy beautiful views over Malhamdale. In the village itself the **Church of St Michael the Archangel** is one of the most attractive in the area, with sheep grazing in the graveyard, and a note in the porch telling you what birds you might expect to see nearby. There has been a church on this site since the 7th or 8th century, the present building dating back to 1490. The bells of the present church are the ones heard by Tom, in *The Water Babies*, as he came down the river. Inside, the register bears the signature of Oliver Cromwell, who witnessed a wedding here, and don't miss the sad wall-plate in the Lambert Chapel, to the right of the altar.

St Michael the Archangel,
Kirkby Malham

Malham Cove

MALHAM

Malham is said to be one of the most visited villages in Britain, and on a summer bank holiday weekend it is indeed like being at Wembley on Cup Final day. The large car park at the **National Park Centre** overflows, and cars are parked all along the verges into the village. Some people like crowds, of course, but if you do want to avoid them then avoid weekends, avoid mid-summer, and try to get there early in any case.

The main attraction isn't the village, which is no prettier than a hundred other Dales villages, but the surrounding scenery. The crowds do at least start to disperse in several different directions. Most head for **Malham Cove**, which is sign-posted from the village and is an easy half-mile walk. But it doesn't matter how crowded it is, it remains a breathtaking sight: a sweep of grey limestone cliff, like a waterfall of rock about 300ft high and 1,000ft long. Comparisons with a waterfall are inevitable, as water did once plunge over these rocks, and what a sight it must have been. The more energetic can clamber up the Cove for a magnificent view of the limestone pavements on top.

The best pub food in Malham is found at the **Lister Arms**. The main bar is large, the service friendly and the beer good – including Pendle Witches Brew. The bar menu varies from sandwiches, steaks and gammon to the unexpected – and delicious – swordfish with parsley butter. There are many other fish dishes, and a wide choice of fresh salads. Meals served daily, except Tuesday. Last orders: lunch 3pm; dinner 11pm.

A *long* uphill walk from Malham will bring you to **Malham Tarn**, and you might be better advised to drive up, then park and walk. As good a place as any to leave a car is by the cattle grid near the entrance to the Field Studies Council centre, marked 'Bridleway, Malham Tarn'. Don't attempt to drive down, it only leads to the centre itself, where parking is restricted to residents only. Past residents, incidentally, have included Charles Kingsley, Charles Darwin and John Ruskin, who were all friends of the former owner, Walter Morrison. Kingsley wrote most of *The Water Babies* while staying at Tarn House, which features in the book along with Malham Cove.

The tarn is a natural lake, the second largest in Yorkshire, covering almost 150 acres. Despite the popularity of nearby Malham, this is an isolated place and thankfully not disturbed by watersports enthusiasts. It is an important refuge for local plant and bird life, having been designated a Site of Special Scientific Interest. There are old woodlands around part of the lake, and elsewhere open moorland. You can take the bridleway and follow it as far as you like round the tarn, the whole journey taking about an hour, with part of it back on the road again. Shortly after the start of the walk, near Tarn House, is a bird hide. This is for anyone to use so don't be shy about going down to it. Malham Tarn is noted for its wildfowl, naturally, but the other birds in the area include peregrine falcons, sparrowhawks, kingfishers and wagtails. The lake is strangely shaped, almost like a shield, and the turns on the paths as you walk round are constantly giving rise to changes in the landscape.

FROM MALHAM TO GORDALE SCAR

An attractive walk takes in **Janet's Foss** and **Gordale Scar**. These two natural features are a few hundred yards from each other, and both can be seen on a very pleasant riverside walk from Malham itself. The start isn't too well sign-posted, but you should follow the path by the river at the National Park Centre end of the village, walking past the front of Miresfield House. The path then becomes easier to follow, over the ladder stiles through the fields by the river, taking care not to head off on the path marked 'Pennine Way'. While walking by the river, under the trees, listen for the rat-tat of the woodpecker and watch out for the blue flash of a kingfisher across the stream. What you're more likely to see are dippers, the little brown birds that look like waiters in best bib and tucker, bobbing up and down on stones in the river.

The path will eventually bring you to the small but attractive fall known as Janet's Foss, with a circular pool in front of it where local shepherds used to dip their sheep. Carry on past here, over the road and through the campsite (it's well marked) to Gordale Scar, a narrow gorge with walls that are 300ft high in places. The path ends at the entrance to the gorge where you'll find a waterfall that varies from a drip to a flood, depending on the season. Many people climb up beside this for a better view of the gorge, but the rocks can be slippery and you do so at your own risk.

There are several ways of returning to Malham from here. The quickest but least appealing is back along the main road, Gordale Lane, where you'll need to watch out for cars and visibility is restricted by high hedges. Slightly longer is to return the way you came, but if you want to extend the walk by perhaps an hour, turn left as you emerge from the campsite that leads to Gordale Scar. This is Hawthorns Lane. When you reach the top of the hill turn right along the Public Bridleway, a walled lane that takes you higher to Weets Top. From this vantage point there are good views of the moorland and the limestone landscape towards Malham. Go through the gate and follow the sign for Windy Pike Lane. After a mile you reach a ladder stile, where you switch to the path marked Hanlith. This path crosses the rough land of Hanlith Moor, and to keep on the path simply pick out the waymark posts with their yellow tops. At the other end of the moor a gate opens onto Windy Pike Lane, which leads into Hanlith and a sign pointing right for the Pennine Way. This then meets up with the path you originally followed through the woods to Janet's Foss.

Janet's Foss, Malham

✪ SKIPTON

Skipton is a busy market town, the market stalls filling both sides of the long High Street, with the Parish Church and Castle at one end, and cobbled streets and alleyways leading off either side. The name Skipton derives from the Anglo-Saxon for Sheep-Town, and part of the thronging High Street is still called Sheep Street. Just behind Sheep Street you'll find the **Tourist Information Office**, at 8 Victoria Square (tel: 0756-792809).

Many towns call themselves the Gateway to the Dales, but Skipton can justify it more than most, with Wharfedale and Malhamdale a few minutes away, and the Leeds-Liverpool canal connecting it to the northern industrial towns whose inhabitants have traditionally escaped to the fresh air of the Dales at week-ends. The canal tow-path provides a very pleasant walk if you want to get out of town, past old terraced cottages through Skipton Woods.

Skipton Market is the biggest in the Dales and is held every day of the week except Tuesday and Sunday, causing crowds, bustle and traffic chaos. Fortunately there's a huge car park behind the Town Hall half-way along the High Street, although even this overflows regularly. The market is excellent for fruit, vegetables, fresh meat and fish, local farmhouse cheeses, clothes and just about everything else.

Skipton Castle

At the top of the High Street stands the **Parish Church of the Holy Trinity**, and it's worth buying the well-produced guidebook to get the most from your visit. It reminds us of something which we perhaps don't consider when looking at the gravestones found beneath our feet in many churches: 'Burial inside this church was popular in the early 1800s, but by the middle of the century the smell was becoming unbearable.' Some parts of the church date back to 1300, notably the Sedilia, the recessed stone seats to the right of the altar where the priest and his assistants used to sit during Mass. The church seems a popular lightning conductor, and several fires are noted. Buried here are the father and other relatives of Lady Anne Clifford, a familiar name in the Dales.

Immediately behind the Parish Church is **Skipton Castle**, which the town boasts is 900 years old and still fully roofed! Lady Anne Clifford turns up again here, as she was born here in 1590 and was largely responsible for rebuilding the castle in the 17th century after it had been very badly damaged by Cromwell's army during the Civil War. It is now one of the best preserved mediaeval castles in the country, and in its central Conduit Court is a magnificent yew tree, planted by Lady Anne at the time of the castle's restoration. No doubt she would be delighted to see it still flourishing, surrounded by visitors admiring the building. Full marks are due to whoever thought of and designed the castle's tour sheet, which is handed out when you enter, as this enables you to do your own guided tour and get the most from your visit. The sheet contains not just written information but drawings, too, which show you where to go next when faced with a choice of several doors. The many castle rooms are all empty of furnishings yet are in a marvellous state of preservation and the kitchens and dungeons are particularly atmospheric.

Skipton Castle. Tel: 0756-792442
Opening times: daily except Christmas Day from 10am (Sun 2pm). Last admission
6pm Apr-Sept, earlier in winter
Admission: adult £2.20; child £1.10

Half-way down the High Street in the Town Hall is the **Craven Museum**. Entry is free, and the exhibits are comprehensively labelled. There are Besom Engines, one of which belonged to 'Besom' Jamie, Queen Victoria's official besom maker. Besoms are long-handled brooms made from twigs, much-favoured by witches. One small display is about Thomas Spencer, one of the founders of Marks and Spencer, who was born in Skipton in 1851. There is also an excellent exhibition of photographs and postcards relating to the First World War, including a hand-written account by a Private Stott of Skipton which describes his experiences as a POW after being captured by the Germans on April 14, 1918. It would be fascinating to be able to read the full account, if it were available as a pamphlet. The most moving items are the 18th-century letters which deal with the question of the Poor Relief of that period. People were only eligible in the parish in which they had been born, so many letters exist from people in the sorriest circumstances, barely literate, pleading for help in the rawest manner imaginable. An interesting collection – and they should do more to promote it.

The Craven Museum. Tel: 0756-790479
Opening times: Apr-Sept: Sat 10am-noon and 1-5pm, Sun 2-5pm, otherwise 11am-
5pm, closed Tues. Oct-Mar: Sat 10am-noon and 1.30-4.30pm, weekdays 2-5pm, closed
Tues and Sun

The stripped pine tables in **Herbs** (10 High Street, Skipton; tel: 0756-60619) give it more the look of a café, but the food is delicious with dishes such as spinach and mushroom flan, tofu burger and chutney and interesting salads, all served with better bread than you'll find in many a smart restaurant. Finish off with hot treacle tart or plum and ginger pie, both served with fresh cream. A good choice of teas includes herbal teas such as nettle or rosehip, or even a dandelion coffee. Open 9.30am-5pm daily, except Tuesday and Sunday.

Embsay Station, almost unchanged since 1888

🏃 A mile from Skipton is the **Embsay Steam Railway**. This is an attempt to recreate the days of steam trains puffing through the Dales, and although the line is only 2½ miles long it still passes through some very attractive craggy scenery. Journeys on the mainly Yorkshire-built steam trains begin and end at Embsay Station, whose exterior is maintained more or less as it has been since 1888. Inside you'll find a small café and a shop well-stocked with railway books and gifts, and model trains. Outside is a small collection of locomotives and carriages, dating back to the 1920s. At present there are other stops at Holywell Halt and Stoneacre Loop, which are pleasant places to picnic or go for a short walk. A service runs from 11am-4.15pm every Sunday throughout the year, on Saturdays and Tuesdays in July, daily in August and all Bank Holidays except Christmas and Boxing Day. For information telephone 0756-794727; for talking timetable telephone 0756-795189.

About five miles outside Skipton, on the A65 beyond Gargrave, watch for the **Coniston Estate Shop** which sells fresh trout and game from the Estate. Meat and game is smoked on the premises, and includes venison, pheasant, quail, duck and pigeon. There are quails' eggs, game pie, venison sausages, oak-smoked trout pâté, swordfish steaks and an enormous range of cheeses. Foodies will faint, and should come armed with a freezer-truck and several credit cards. Open daily, 10am-6pm (tel: 0756-748136).

WHERE TO STAY

Bolton Abbey
🏠 ✕ 🏃 🐎 🍽 **££££**

Devonshire Arms Hotel, *Bolton Abbey, Skipton, N Yorks BD23 6AJ*
Tel: 0756-710441
Open all year
This small but lavish country hotel, hidden in trees on the edge of Bolton Abbey Estate, looks like a Georgian gentleman's residence. Most of the furniture and paintings belong to the owners, the Duke and Duchess of Devonshire. All rooms are spacious with antique tables and bureaus, Victorian-style wallpaper, a mixture of brass and canopied beds, and every convenience the modern traveller expects. Smart dress is preferred in the restaurant, where starters include a salad of avocado, paw-paw and mangetout dressed with a sorrel and hazelnut vinaigrette. There is an optional intermediate course before reaching the main course, perhaps baked layers of salmon, oysters and mushrooms on a champagne and salmon caviare sauce. Last orders: lunch 1.45pm; dinner 9.45pm.

Gargrave

⌂ 🚶 ✉ ££

Eshton Grange, *Gargrave, near Skipton, N Yorks BD23 3QE*
Tel: 0756-749383
Open all year

By the side of a quiet country road, Eshton Grange is an 18th-century listed farmhouse with 20 acres of land, a Shetland pony stud, any number of farm animals and free-range hens. Behind the house is a lovingly tended private walled garden, with croquet lawn and garden furniture. The four bedrooms vary enormously, although all are spacious with lots of lovely old-fashioned furniture. There's a top floor family apartment, which children will love as the beds are on a platform under the beams, reached by ladder. Dinner is available, with hearty home-cooking needing a good appetite. The owners, Judy and Terry Shelmerdine, couldn't be more accommodating, making guests feel that nothing is too much trouble.

Grassington

⌂ 🚶5 ✉ ££

Ashfield House, *off Main Street, Grassington, Skipton, N Yorks BD23 5AE*
Tel: 0756-752584
Closed January

A delightful and quiet 17th-century building down a cul-de-sac off Grassington's busy Main Street, Ashfield House has open fires in the two lounges and a lot of stripped pine in its seven double bedrooms, five with en suite bathrooms. Guests have the use of a drying room, for wet walking days. The hotel is licensed, and the owners prefer guests to stay for dinner. The menu includes produce grown in the huge walled garden. A typical menu could include carrot and coriander soup, gammon steak in a raisin sauce, home-made rum and raisin ice-cream, a selection of local cheeses and coffee and mints, with perhaps pâté made from garden herbs as a vegetarian option.

Kettlewell

⌂ 🚶8 🐴 ▭ £££

Dale House Country Hotel, *Kettlewell, N Yorks BD23 5QZ*
Tel: 0756-760836
Open all year

A large detached stone house, the late 19th-century Dale House has lovely views over Wharfedale. Some of the six rooms have showers, some baths, one even has a Jacuzzi and four-poster bed. While there are the usual problems of squeezing en suite facilities into rooms not designed for them, the bedrooms still have plenty of space. The owners, Tony and Anne Butterfield, are affable and informative, having produced a leaflet for guests listing local walks and drives. Other little touches include a filled flask available with the packed lunch, home-made biscuits and fresh fruit in the rooms. Food is home-cooked, and a typical menu might comprise pâté of minced mushroom cooked in claret, roast shoulder of Yorkshire lamb with a rosemary and white wine sauce and home-made banana cream syllabub.

Malham

⌂ 🚶 🐴 ✉ ££

Miresfield Farm, *Malham, Skipton, N Yorks BD23 4DA*
Tel: 0729-830414
Open all year

Now a farm in name only, this detached house on the edge of Malham with its rambling corridors has 14 bedrooms. Often a busy, convivial place, popular with walkers, it's very economically priced. Set beside the village stream and with a large and colourful garden, the views from many of the rooms of the surrounding Malhamdale countryside are exceptional. The owners, Peter and Vera Sharp, are hospitable local people who are often to be found with the guests in one of the two lounges. Bedrooms are basically furnished but all are clean and obviously looked after. There's a large and light stone-walled oak-beamed dining room, where the food is simple hearty farmhouse cooking.

Skipton

🏠 🎿 🛏 **£££**

Oats Hotel and Restaurant, *Chapel Hill, Skipton, N Yorks BD23 1NL*
Tel: 0756-68118
Open all year
Oats has an ideal location, a minute's walk from the castle and parish church, but set back in a quiet cul-de-sac. There are only five characterful rooms, each impeccably decorated with thick carpets and superior furnishings. Yet although the rooms are luxurious, they don't omit those personal touches that matter, such as fresh milk for morning tea. The lounges are large, fresh flowers and bright paintings abound, and the restaurant is also highly commended. There are two fixed-price menus, with a wide choice of about seven dishes for each course. Starters might include quail, fillets of brill or terrine of local rabbit, with a second course of soup, sorbet or salad, followed by trout, lamb, hake or duck.

WHERE TO EAT

Gargrave

✗ 🛏 **££**

The Kettle Restaurant, *60-62 High Street, Gargrave, near Skipton*
Tel: 0756-749252
Open daily, closed Tues lunch
This is another of the many Dales family restaurants producing first-class food at reasonable prices. There are three fixed-price menus and to compensate for the lack of choice within them you can choose between them and adjust the price. The Kettle is also happy to cook any dish to order, given sufficient notice. The food tends to be straightforward and traditional, with good ingredients, prepared and presented with great attention to detail. An escalope of salmon is served on a tempting bed of tomato and chive butter sauce, while even on the basic menu the pan-fried strips of beef fillet come with a basil, onion, tomato and pine kernel sauce. Last orders: lunch 2.30pm; dinner 9.30pm.

Grassington

✕ ▭ ££

Number Forty Seven, *47 Main Street, Grassington*
Tel: 0756-752069
Open daily
Number Forty Seven is the type of place which seldom makes the culinary guides, being an ordinary and unpretentious little restaurant, yet it has an informal atmosphere and offers good plain home cooking at remarkably reasonable prices. It has an ambitious menu, each course with a dozen or so options, yet the bustle that comes from the kitchen suggests that meals are freshly prepared. Starters include kidneys in madeira, home-made pâtés and soups, with main courses such as pork fillets in a grainy mustard sauce or chicken breasts in a wine, cream and mushroom sauce. The summer pudding is substantial and delicious, the wine list wide and economically priced. Last orders: lunch 1.30pm; dinner 9pm.

Hetton

✕ ▭ ££

The Angel Inn, *Hetton, near Skipton*
Tel: 0756-73263
Open Mon-Sat dinner only, Sun lunch only
A visit to the Angel is a must, but needs pre-booking or a little pre-planning as it's justifiably popular. You can book in the restaurant, but in the bar it's first come, first served. The waiters seem to be mostly good-natured Yorkshire lads, who evidently relish the bustle. The food is wonderful: gravadlax, confit of duck served with a blood orange and curaçao sauce or brochette of pork with peppers, onions and wild rice appear on both menus. In the bar this means restaurant quality food at bar prices, and the chance to sample one of the many fine-quality wines that are available by the glass. Last orders: lunch 2pm; dinner 9.30pm.

Threshfield

🍽 ✉ ££

The Old Hall, *Threshfield*
Tel: 0756-752441
Open daily; closed Mon Jan-May
A large roadside inn, the Old Hall has been modernised without losing its oak-panelling and atmospheric dim light. You can dine in the main bar, which has many nooks and crannies, though here you may have a long wait for a table as the good cooking and economical prices have made it extremely popular. There is also a dining area to one side, and a slightly more formal conservatory restaurant. The menu is similar in all three places, and the Old Hall has carved a niche for itself by offering good food from around the world. The chicken may be curried, in the form of Chinese-style chicken wings, or plain English roasted. The beer is better than the wine, and the quality of the cooking raises it well above the 'pub grub' label.

YORKSHIRE DALES NATIONAL PARK CENTRES

There are six National Park Centres, which are open from April to October and provide maps, books, leaflets, postcards and general information about every aspect of the National Park. They also organise guided walks throughout the season, and these are strongly recommended. They range from general introductory walks with a warden, dealing with a particular area, to walks with an expert on a specific subject, whether it be lead-mining or botany. The dates and details obviously change from year to year, so do look out for details at the centres themselves, or at Tourist Information Centres, which are frequently in the same building. There are also Activity Days for Children, for ages 7-12, with or without their parents.

For information on particular areas of the National Park, contact Aysgarth Falls (tel: 0969-663424); Clapham (tel: 05242-51419); Grassington (tel: 0756-752774); Hawes (tel: 0969-667450); Malham (tel: 0729-830363); Sedbergh (tel: 05396-20125).

The National Park also offers a 24-hour Weathercall service, in conjunction with the Meteorological Office, on 0891-500748.

For general information about the Yorkshire Dales National Park, contact the head office: The Yorkshire Dales National Park, Colvend, Hebden Road, Grassington, Skipton, North Yorkshire BD23 5LB (tel: 0756-752748).

ILKLEY MOOR AND HAWORTH

This is the region of Wharfedale and Airedale, two dales which change character as they head towards the more built-up parts of south Yorkshire. Around Ilkley the land is still wooded in places, the town itself a more cosmopolitan version of a typical Dales market town. As you go south you'll find a more sprawling look as the land flattens into moorland and villages give way to towns, increasingly running into each other. By the time you reach Haworth, you know you're leaving the true Dales behind, though few can resist the drive round Ilkley Moor to see the town and landscape of Emily Brontë's *Wuthering Heights*.

Haworth is the biggest tourist attraction in Yorkshire, and it's worth joining the international crowds to see it. Old Haworth is an attractive village of climbing cobbled streets and a good place for a family day out, wet or dry. There are small museums that will appeal to children, as well as Brontë Parsonage for the adults. Nearby are East Riddlesden Hall and Cliffe Castle, the former a delightful 17th-century house, the latter a first-rate museum and park. Families can also ride on the Keighley and Worth Valley Railway, which stops at Haworth and at Oxenhope, with its railway museum. If the day is fine then stroll round the pleasant market towns of Ilkley and Otley. If you're really energetic take a walk on the famous Ilkley Moor to find the Twelve Apostles, the Swastika Stone and the Cow and Calf Rocks... then treat yourself to something at Betty's tea rooms afterwards.

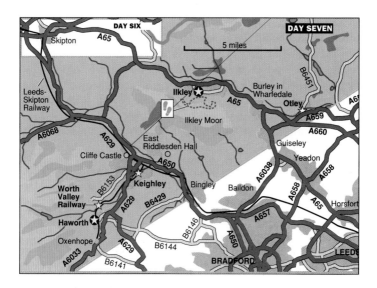

✪ HAWORTH

Haworth was once an isolated community of weavers and despite the crowds its rugged beauty can still be admired. It now sprawls a little untidily at the edges, like many of the increasingly industrialised towns in this part of Yorkshire, but the original village is still there, and at its heart is the beautiful Main Street. This is steep, cobbled and lined mainly with solid, grey-brown, stone Victorian cottages, although many of these two-up-two-down homes are now open as tea rooms and little shops catering to the tourist trade. At the top of Main Street is the Old Apothecary, which is a true measure of change as a sign outside explains that this was once the Druggist Store, where Bronwell Brontë used to buy his opium: credit cards now accepted.

Haworth is almost famous for being famous. It has become a kind of literary Blackpool, the Stratford of the North, its streets crammed with people who probably wouldn't know Emily Brontë from Emily Bishop. In fact *Wuthering Heights* meets *Coronation Street* just about sums the place up. And yet you have to go, if only once. The Haworth **Tourist Information Centre** is at 2/4 West Lane (tel: 0535-642329).

What was once the imposing and gloomy parsonage of the Reverend Patrick Brontë is now the **Brontë Parsonage Museum**, devoted to the life and works of his famous children: Charlotte, Emily, Anne and Branwell. (Two other children, Maria and Elizabeth, died in childhood, not long after their mother.) The forbidding building looks out over the graveyard of the Parish Church, while inside most of the rooms have been restored, as far as possible, to what they looked like when the Brontës were in residence from 1820 until the end of their lives.

Like iron filings round a magnet, the tourists mill around the entrance and the small rooms, some partly roped off. All jostle to see the room where Emily Brontë died at the age of only 30, the writing desks, the manuscripts, the paintings of Branwell and a plethora of Brontë-owned artefacts, many housed in the rather more spacious Exhibition and Library wing built on in the 1870s. There is no quiet time to visit, but being first through the door in the morning is about as quiet as it gets.

Brontë Parsonage Museum. Tel: 0535-642323
Opening times: daily Apr-Sept 10am-5pm, Oct-Mar 11am-4.30pm; closed Jan 21-Feb 8 and Dec 24-26
Admission: adult £2.50; child 50p

Directly in front of the Museum, on the other side of the cemetery, is the **Haworth Parish Church**. This attracts more visitors than the average church, but nevertheless it's a haven of peace and quiet compared to the rest of Haworth. Those that do manage to divert themselves by a few yards to find the church seem to take a quick peep at the Brontë Memorial and move on, but there are other attractions. There is some beautiful stained glass, especially the Taylor Window, showing the Twelve Apostles and members of the Taylor family who commissioned it. Underneath the East 'Te Deum' Window is a lovely detailed Italian alabaster relief, based on Leonardo da Vinci's Last Supper. Don't miss Charlotte Brontë's marriage certificate or Patrick Brontë's 17th-century Bible, although you must remember that the church is

Brontë Parsonage Museum and Parish Church Graveyard, Haworth

not the building in which Patrick Brontë actually preached. Only the tower now remains, the rest having been pulled down and rebuilt by Patrick Brontë's successor, a Reverend Wade, perhaps to rid himself of the Brontë mythology which had already come into existence. The churchyard is also worth visiting, containing memorials to some 40,000 villagers and the graves of Brontë servants Tabitha Aykroys and Martha Brown. The Brontës themselves are all buried in a crypt beneath the church, with the exception of Anne who died in Scarborough.

Where else would you want to have lunch in Haworth, other than **The Black Bull** on Main Street, the pub where Branwell Brontë was a regular? Unfortunately everyone else has the same idea. However, if you get there early enough and grab one of the all-too-few tables you'll get a good pub lunch. The service is remarkably efficient and the prices fair. The menu includes lasagne, chilli con carne and mixed grills, with daily specials such as beef in red wine, chicken in white wine or bacon chops, served with all the trimmings. Meals are served daily from noon until early evening.

Haworth is into nostalgia in a big way, and though **Bygone Days** looks none too exciting from the outside (like the back end of the old cinema it once was), inside is an Aladdin's cave of memorabilia. What makes the museum different is that many of the exhibits have been used as props in television series and films. You'll see items from *Rising Damp*, *Watching*, *In Loving Memory* and the movie *Yanks*, amongst others. Fans of *Emmerdale* can see Amos' tricycle and Seth's aged bike and trailer, and many of the exhibits are still hired out to series like *Last of the Summer Wine*. This programme, incidentally, is filmed 20 miles to the south, in Holmfirth, on the edge of the Peak District and not in the Yorkshire Dales as is commonly believed. Downstairs, the one-time cinema stalls are now a cobbled street with toy shops, chemists and general stores, all crammed with goods. They are described as 'period', which encompasses every period from Victorian to about the 1950s, and are none the worse for that. Upstairs more shops surround the balconies, and the very pleasant Old Court Café serves light snacks. It's good to see a private enterprise like this which caters for the disabled, with seating for about 20 disabled people, toilet facilities and reduced admission.

Bygone Days, Belle Isle Road, Haworth. Tel: 0535-646424
Opening times: 11am-5pm every Sat and Sun, also Wednes, Easter-Oct, and all Bank Hols except Dec 24-26. Ring for confirmation as it is hoped that opening hours will increase
Admission: adult £1.50; child 50p

Attracting children and adults in equal numbers, and based in what was once the Haworth Liberal Club, **The Museum of Childhood** doesn't yet seem to have found adequate premises to allow itself to put on a good display. The admission price should be halved, when compared to other attractions, but if visiting Haworth it would be hard to resist seeing this collection of toys that have been squirrelled away over the years by a couple of collectors. Here are dozens of dolls, from Victorian to punk, and train set layouts where the trains all run at the push of a button. There's bound to be something to enable you to say: 'I had one of those'. There are also collections of teddy bears, dinky toys, dolls' houses, Meccano sets and card games. Nostalgia behind glass.

Museum of Childhood, Main Street, Haworth. Tel: 0535-643593
Opening times: daily Apr-Oct, Nov-Mar weekends and school holidays only, 10.30am-5.30pm
Admission: adult £1; child 50p

✪ ILKLEY

Ilkley is famous now for its moor, but at one time it was, like Harrogate, a popular spa town with visitors coming to take the waters and then stride out over Ilkley Moor. This is the moor which, according to the old dialect song, you have to walk on b'aht 'at, or without a hat in plain English. Sometimes regarded as the Yorkshire national anthem, the words are traditionally believed to have been composed by a Halifax church choir who were having a very merry picnic beneath the moor's Cow and Calf Rocks. There was once a Bull Rock too, but the stone was used to help build the Crescent Hotel. If you want to walk further than the moor, Ilkley is the starting point for the Dales Way which leads to the Lake District.

Ilkley has many other attractions, not least for those who like their food. In addition to the renowned Box Tree Inn, providing the best gourmet food in the Dales (see Where to Eat), there is one of Betty's famous tea rooms and several good but affordable bistros. It is also a busy shopping centre, with glass-canopied shops selling books and antiques, and a relaxed appealing atmosphere. The Ilkley **Tourist Information Centre** is in Station Road, Ilkley, West Yorkshire LS29 8HA (tel: 0943-602319).

In The Grove, a canopied parade of shops in the town centre, Ilkley's **Betty's** is a smaller place than its Harrogate sister, with more restricted opening hours (9am-6pm Monday-Thursday, 9am-7.30pm Friday-Sunday). It has the same menus, though, and a shop at the front sells most of Betty's fine foodstuffs: delicious fattening dishes such as apple strudel and cream, fruit cheesecake or Yorkshire curd tart and cream. If it's bad for you, Betty's serves it.

The Manor House Museum is a fine beamed building in a courtyard behind the Parish Church, though as a museum it's disappointingly small when compared to the packed collections housed in Dales towns only a quarter the size. In fact the building itself is of more interest than what's inside, dating back to the 16th century and thought to have been either the Vicarage or a yeoman farmer's house. There is an exhibition of furniture representing a yeoman's house of that period, and a feature to watch out for is the 17th-century wall privy. Inside you'll also find a small display featuring *that* song, 'On Ilkley Moor B'Aht 'At', as well as the usual potted history of the town. Downstairs rooms contain the paltry local history collection, while upstairs a more enterprising gallery hosts art and crafts exhibitions.

The Manor House Museum, Castle Yard. Tel: 0943-600066
Opening times: Tues-Sun, 10am-6pm (closes at 5pm Oct-Mar); closed Mon except
Bank Hols⁻
Admission: free

Manor House Museum, Ilkley

Next to the museum, the **Parish Church of All Saints** is worth seeing, particularly for some lovely stained glass windows. There has been a church on this site overlooking the River Wharfe since the 7th century, and the present church has several interesting features from across the centuries: Saxon crosses, a 13th-century doorway, a 14th-century effigy of a local knight and one of the very few 17th-century box pews still surviving. The font is made of stone from Ilkley Moor, the date being uncertain but certainly pre-mediaeval. The stained glass includes the Four Marys' window, designed in 1922 by the William Morris Gallery, and the east window is beautiful Flemish glass from 1860, depicting the Crucifixion.

Parish Church of All Saints, Ilkley

ON ILKLEY MOOR B'AHT 'AT

No one can possibly visit Ilkley without at least taking a look at the famous Ilkley Moor, but if you have time get out on to it: this circular walk of between three and four hours takes in most of the main features.

If starting from the town centre, head for the railway station and walk up Wells Road, next to the Midland Bank. Alternatively you can drive up and park in a small car park just over the cattle grid at the very top of Wells Road. Across the road from here you can see the first point of interest, a group of white buildings known as the White Wells, so follow the marked track as far as here.

These were the original open-air spa baths, founded in the mid-18th century and leading to the town's popularity as a resort. The medicinal properties of the local waters are said to have been realised when a local shepherd fell on the moor and injured his leg, which was helped to recovery after being bathed in the spring. A staircase leads down to one of the baths which has recently been restored, and note the small set of steps outside, to enable ladies to mount the donkeys which took them back into town.   →

From the White Wells take the path going up towards a small clump of trees, which then veers to the left below an escarpment. Keep heading east until the path forks, and take the left-hand path into what's known as Rocky Valley. You could almost be in the Wild West, with the rocks towering above you, but in fact you're still quite close to Ilkley town and have hardly ventured on to the moor. Follow the path through the valley to a large boulder, from where you can see the **Cow and Calf Rocks** in the distance below you – and there should be no mistaking these two prominent features! Walk down to these crossing a stream on the way, and enjoy a scramble around the rocks, from the top of which there are wonderful views of Ilkley and the distant dales.

Cow and Calf Rocks, Ilkley Moor

With the town at your back and the path from Rocky Valley on your right, head for the crest of the hill, across a stream. Then follow the well-marked path to the top of Ilkley Crags. You should now be above the escarpment you recently walked beneath. Below you are two tarns, these being the footsteps of the giant, Rombald, who was chased by his wife across Ilkley Moor. It's said he tripped over one large rock and chipped a piece off, and that's how the Cow and Calf Rocks were formed. Pay attention now to the modern giants, the two large radio masts of Whetstone Gate, which you should be heading towards along the path. Keep to the higher path, well left of a group of pine trees.

The path crosses a stream, and beyond that meets the rough track which leads up to the masts. Ignore this track and press on ahead, through some bracken, walking parallel to the reservoir you can see on the edge of Ilkley below you. As you come to a stream, Heber's Ghyll, don't cross it but follow it down until you meet a track at right-angles to it. Turn left here towards the railings which surround another of Ilkley Moor's features, the **Swastika Stone**. This is a Bronze Age rock carving whose purpose is still a mystery, but it resembles others found in Sweden and Italy and is believed to be Yorkshire's oldest rock carving.

From the Swastika Stone you need to walk back along the same path, over Heber's Ghyll, along the top of the reservoir, and keep to the right of the woods beyond the reservoir. A well-used path leads from here back down to the road that goes up to Whetstone Gate. Turn left, then right at the next T-junction to get back to the car park. An invigorating introduction to Ilkley Moor. If it's sunny, you can even do it b'aht 'at.

☆ KEIGHLEY

Between Ilkley and Haworth lies Keighley, a typical gritty Yorkshire industrial town, more noted for rugby league than for culture. Yet images are often misleading, of course, and while no one would pretend that Keighley is beautiful, it is worth visiting Cliffe Castle Museum and gardens, taking a ride on the Worth Valley Railway, and also seeing, on the edge of the town, the National Trust's East Riddlesden Hall.

Keighley is also a good place to visit some of Yorkshire's famous **Factory Shops** selling good quality goods at trade prices. The largest is Peter Black on Lawkholme Lane (tel: 0535-661177), open Monday-Saturday, 9am-5.30pm. The shop carries a good stock of a very wide range of items, including furniture and bedding, shoes, coats, jackets, bags and luggage.

M D Fabrics on South Street (tel: 0535-664206) opens 10am-5pm on weekdays, except Tuesday when it's closed, and on Saturdays from 10am-1pm. More a specialist shop for dressmakers, it sells woollen, cotton and polyester fabrics, linings and some partly-made skirts ready to sew. It doesn't sell ready-to-wear items, but you can find some of those a short walk away at the Springfield Mill Shop (tel: 0535-606600) on Oakworth Road. This is open Monday-Saturday, 9am-5pm, and sells just about any garment you can think of, catering for men, women and children.

Cliffe Castle is a grand late 19th-century mansion, built by a local wool baron, Henry Butterfield. Set in a wooded park overlooking Keighley, with aviaries and a children's play area, its museum is a wonderful mix of ancient and modern. Both are represented in the high-tech Molecules to Minerals gallery which has a large collection of rocks and minerals, strikingly lit to look appealing and exciting. There's also a life-size model of a newt, which may not sound too special, but this creature, once found in the area, is the size of a small dinosaur. Upstairs there are stuffed animals, birds' nests, stained glass, Hoovers, Elvis Presley album covers, jelly moulds, old toys galore and a working bee-hive, the bees crawling in through a glass pipe connected to the outside. There are also some elegant furnished rooms from the days of Henry Butterfield, and space is given over to touring exhibitions.

Cliffe Castle Museum and Gardens, Keighley. Tel: 0274-758230
Opening times: open Tues-Sun 10am-6pm (closes at 5pm Oct-Mar); closed Good Fri,
Christmas Day, Boxing Day and Mon except Bank Hols
Admission: free

Cliffe Castle Museum, Keighley

 East Riddlesden Hall is a 17th-century building set in 12 acres of land, though in this more urban part of Yorkshire it lacks the grand vistas of country houses elsewhere. It doesn't lack history, however, as the Manor of Riddlesden goes back to at least 1086, when it was owned by the Lord of Bingley. In the 1630s James Murgatroyd bought the land and what was probably a building dating back to mediaeval times. This he renovated and extended, and much of it remains for the visitor to see.

Outside is a delightful walled garden and a fishpond which is referred to by the monks of Bolton Priory in 1320. In front of the house is a very well preserved mediaeval barn, which you ought not to miss for its dimly lit interior which at once conjures up pictures of merrie England and the noise of workmen.

Inside is a series of varied and fascinating rooms. One is the Grey Lady's Chamber, named after the ghostly figure said to have been seen around the house on several occasions, whilst the two most interesting rooms are the Great Hall – with a fireplace in which you could roast an ox – and the Kitchen. The latter contains a recipe for cooking and serving a peacock! The Hall has a gift shop and a spacious tearoom serving light lunches. These, the barn and part of the grounds can all be visited for free. On Mondays, Tuesdays and Wednesdays the admission charge includes guided tours between noon and 2pm. At other times there is a guide in almost every room to answer questions.

East Riddlesden Hall, Bradford Road, Keighley. Tel: 0535-607075
Opening times: noon-5.30pm, last admissions 5pm: Mar-Apr, Easter and weekends only; May-Oct, Sat-Wednes
Admission: adult £2; child £1; NT members free

East Riddlesden Hall, Keighley

The attractions of **The Keighley and Worth Valley Railway** are divided among the various stations along its five miles of track, which link Keighley Station on the Leeds-Settle-Carlisle line with the villages of the Worth Valley. The line was first opened in 1867 by a company formed mainly of local mill owners, and after closure in 1961 it was re-opened by steam train enthusiasts in 1968. Since then it has run a service every weekend and daily during the summer with a trip from Keighley at one end to Oxenhope at the other taking only 25 minutes. The trains are mostly small Thomas-the-Tank-Engine types, and the carriages have been lovingly restored, though what you travel in varies according to what happens to be in service. If you are lucky, you might ride in the luxury of an old Pullman car. Another old-fashioned feature is Damems, England's smallest fully operational station, and a request stop only. Anyone wanting to leave the train here must inform the guard, and if you want to board tell the station staff, who will stop the train for you.

At Haworth Station the Locomotive Works allows enthusiasts to see the restoration work being done on the old steam trains, and a connecting bus service takes passengers up the steep hill to Haworth's Old Village. The Railway Museum is at Oxenhope. Admission is by giving a donation to the society's funds, and this allows you to wander freely round this collection of old railway engines and general railway memorabilia – signs like 'Buses for Butlins Camp', 'The Brontës at Haworth' and 'None but company's horses allowed to drink at this trough'. A raised platform allows you to peer inside a Pullman car, and you can also stand on the footplate of The Green Dragon, the train used in the film of *The Railway Children*. Other stations include Oakworth, where much of the film was made, and Ingrow West, an old station moved stone by stone from Lancashire. This stop has the most extensive parking if you want to leave your car and travel on the train: an all-day Rover ticket allows you to visit every stop if you wish.

The Keighley and Worth Valley Railway. Tel: 0535-645214 (enquiries) and 0535-643629 (talking timetable)
Opening times: weekends all year round, plus weekdays at Easter and end June - mid-Sept, and Bank Hols. Trains run roughly hourly, from 9.20am at weekends and from about 11.50am weekdays
All-day Rover ticket: adult £4.50; child £2.25

☆ OTLEY

Otley has no single attraction that demands a visit, yet a few hours can be pleasantly spent here. The Otley Agricultural Show dates back to 1796, and is held on the Saturday before the Spring Bank Holiday. The Otley Carnival takes place on the third Saturday in June, while a Victorian Fayre is held in early December. The **Tourist Information Centre** is in the Council Offices at 8 Boroughgate (tel: 0943-465151).

> The town of Guiseley isn't in the Dales, but who could resist a small detour to eat at the most famous fish and chip shop in the world? The dining room of **Harry Ramsden's** is large and light, with some windows looking out over Ilkley Moor, but there's no booking so you have to take pot luck. The menu is simple, consisting of haddock, plaice or halibut, all dipped in batter from Ramsden's secret recipe and served with chips, mushy peas, bread and butter and tea. Cheap and filling, just as it has been since 1931. There's no proper address, but they're by the White Cross on the outskirts of Guiseley, on the main road heading for Otley. Or just follow your nose. Open every day, from 11.30am-10.30pm.

Otley holds several weekly markets. There is a general market every Friday and Saturday, and also on Monday during the summer, and, as well as being good for local produce such as cheese and meat, it has some bric-a-brac and secondhand book stalls. Also on Mondays and Fridays there are two lively cattle markets, especially when Yorkshire TV turns up to film scenes for *Emmerdale* . The Bridge End Auction Mart, at the northern end of the bridge over the River Wharfe, becomes Hotten Market for television purposes. The other market is the Wharfedale Auction Mart, slightly out of town along the Leeds Road, at the foot of the Chevin, a huge, wooded, wild park on a ridge to the south of Otley, and worth seeing for splendid views over Wharfedale.

All Saints' Parish Church is a mainly Norman church, most parts dating from the 11th to the 15th centuries, and inside are some Anglian Crosses which have been dated even further back, to 750AD. The various designs on these, including the mythical Wyvern (a kind of viper representing the devil) were used for teaching and preaching. There are also several lovely Victorian stained glass windows. An unusual feature in the graveyard is a memorial to 30 men who died during construction of a tunnel on the Leeds-Harrogate line, built as a replica of its entrance.

In Market Place is the **Black Bull Inn**, a busy but enjoyable place to have a pub lunch, especially on market days. Expect the usual pub mix of home-made pies, soups, chicken and fish, but the old timbered interior and a roaring fire in winter make it worth a visit. You will be eating and drinking in the same place, according to legend, as Oliver Cromwell's troops, who are said during the Civil War to have drunk the pub dry on the night before the Battle of Marston Moor. Food is served daily, including Sundays, at lunchtime only. Last orders: 2pm.

WHERE TO STAY

Haworth

Old White Lion Hotel, *Main Street, Haworth, Keighley, W Yorks BD22 8DU*
Tel: 0535-42313
Open all year
The accommodation provided in this 300-year-old inn is superior to the average pub with rooms. The 14 bedrooms are spacious, all with en suite bathrooms, though the decor is very simple and functional. Several rooms have extensive views over the nearby moors. There's an oak-panelled lounge reserved for residents, and you can eat in the candlelit restaurant or at the bar. The restaurant is pleasantly old-fashioned, with its timber-framed walls and oak furnishings, and offers good wholesome meals.

Haworth

The Rydings Country Hotel, *Bridgehouse Lane, Haworth, near Keighley, W Yorks BD22 8QE*
Tel: 0535-645206/646933
Open all year
A country house in the heart of Haworth, set back from the main road, its Georgian exterior belies the modern rooms inside, which tend more to stripped pine than oak dresser. All rooms have an office desk and chair, hair-dryer and satellite TV. You may not need the photocopy or fax facilities, but you will appreciate the stained-glass windows on the stairways and the general comfort of the place. It's only a short walk from the centre of Haworth, although up

quite a steep hill. The speciality of the bar is its large selection of fine whiskies, while the restaurant concentrates on English cooking with many traditional Yorkshire dishes.

Ilkley
G ⻌ ✉ ££

Moorview Guest House, *104 Skipton Road, Ilkley, W Yorks LS29 9HE*
Tel: 0943-600156
Open all year
This large Victorian house is on the main through route for traffic but isn't noisy, being well back from the road with plenty of parking space in front. On the opposite side of town from *the* moor, rear rooms do have lovely countryside views across the River Wharfe. Full marks for friendliness and helpfulness from the owner and her small staff, but some rooms need refurbishing and are really only suitable for a short stay, though others are large, spacious and well furnished.

Ilkley
⌂ ✕ ⻌ ⻗ ⊟ ££££

Rombald's Hotel, *West View, Wells Road, Ilkley, W Yorks LS29 9JG*
Tel: 0943-603201
Open all year; Rombald's Restaurant closed Sun dinner
In a row of elegant town houses on tree-lined Wells Road, regular visitors to this award-winning hotel include Ted Heath and Roy Hattersley. There are 15 spacious, tastefully decorated rooms, though some have only showers in bathrooms. The owner, Ian Guthrie, retired from business to create the kind of hotel he always wished he could have stayed in. The result is efficiency combined with friendly attention. The restaurant is not overly expensive given the quality of food. Starters might include rabbit terrine or crab timbale, while main courses may be medallions of venison in a raspberry sauce or baked halibut cooked with a herb crust on a langoustine sauce. The sweet-toothed can have a selection of all the puddings, such as iced orange and aniseed soufflé in a Grand Marnier sauce. Last orders: lunch 2pm; dinner 10pm.

Keighley
⌂ ⻌ ⻗ ⊟ ££

Dalesgate Hotel, *406 Skipton Road, Utley, Keighley, W Yorks BD20 6HP*
Tel: 0535-664930
Open all year; R dinner only
This large Victorian house with its more modern extension caters for a mixture of businessmen and tourists. The 22 bedrooms are compact but pleasant and modern, decorated mostly in plain pinks and limes. There's a very relaxing bar with cane tables and chairs, and the restaurant has a warm country feel. The extensive menu ranges from simple fare such as pork chops with apple sauce or sirloin steaks to fancier dishes such as baked trout in cream and port sauce with garlic and mixed herbs or breast of chicken with an orange, tarragon and shallot sauce and served with orange segments. Last orders: 11pm.

WHERE TO EAT

Haworth
☒ ▭ ££

Weaver's, *15 West Lane, Haworth*
Tel: 0535-643822
Closed: lunch (except winter Suns); Sun dinner; Mon dinner Oct-May

Originally a group of traditional cottages, Weaver's has a cosy, intimate atmosphere. It is popular with locals, having earned a reputation for good Northern cooking. Steak and chips and Pennine pot pie are offered alongside dishes such as breast of duck served with an apple pancake and rhubarb sauce, or breast of chicken stuffed with cream cheese, herbs and a touch of garlic. Fresh fish dishes and vegetarian choices vary daily. Starters range from Yorkshire pudding to peppered strawberry salad, and puddings from old school pudding with custard to a rich chocolate mousse. Last orders: 9.15pm.
Weaver's also has several comfortable guest rooms.

Ilkley
✕ ▭ ££££

The Box Tree Inn, *Church Street, Ilkley*
Tel: 0943-608484
Closed Sun/Mon dinner, Mon lunch

The best food in the Dales... and among the best restaurants in the country. From the outside little more than a box on the main road through Ilkley, inside the decor is a cross between a curry house and the British Museum. There seem to be at least two staff for each customer. You pay for the attention as well as the food – but what food: a terrine of

guinea fowl and chicken with morels and pistachio, or a more simple ravioli of shellfish to start. A melody of sea fish with leeks and caviar might sound over-lyrical, but the cuts of fish are superb, as is the noisette of lamb with jus of tarragon. Puddings include 'The Inimitable Timbale of Strawberries', on the menu many years and regarded by this diner at least as the best pudding he has ever eaten. Last orders: lunch 2pm; dinner 9.45pm.

Ilkley
✕ ▭ ££

Sous-le-Nez, *19 Church Street, Ilkley*
Tel: 0943-600566
Closed Sun

This busy wine bar and brasserie does well with its cheap, enterprising 'early bird' menu served until 2pm and 7.30pm, including a half-bottle of wine. There are three choices for each of three courses and standards are impressive. Perhaps deep-fried camembert in a raspberry dressing or chorizo sausage with apple and onion to start, followed by steamed salmon with leeks and ginger or fillets of pork wrapped in puff pastry with chicken livers and sage. Puddings may include crème brûlée or summer pudding. The à la carte menu also has a wide choice for vegetarians and vegans, one of the owners being a vegetarian. The tables are slightly cramped and you might find a neighbour's elbow *sous* your own *nez*, but the quality of the food is excellent. Last orders: lunch 2.30pm; dinner 10.30pm.